FOR LANCELOT ANDREWES

FOR
LANCELOT ANDREWES

ESSAYS ON STYLE AND ORDER

BY

T. S. ELIOT

"Thou,

Lord, Who walkest in the midst

of the golden candlesticks, remove not,

we pray Thee, our candlestick out its

place; but set in order the things which

are wanting among us, and strengthen

those which remain, and are

ready to die."

GARDEN CITY, N. Y.

1929

DOUBLEDAY, DORAN

AND COMPANY, INC.

For My Mother

PREFACE

HAD I WISHED TO PUBLISH A VOLUME OF COL-
lected literary essays, this book would have
been much bigger. The reader may be puzzled
to know why I selected these articles and in this
order. I wished to indicate certain lines of
development, and to disassociate myself from
certain conclusions which have been drawn
from my volume of essays, *The Sacred Wood.*
To make my present position clear I have three
small books in preparation which will not be
ready for a considerable time. Meanwhile, I
have made bold to unite these occasional essays
merely as an indication of what may be expected, and to refute any accusation of playing
'possum. The general point of view may be
described as classicist in literature, royalist in
politics, and anglo-catholic in religion. I am
quite aware that the first term is completely
vague, and easily lends itself to clap-trap; I
am aware that the second term is at present
without definition, and easily leads itself to
what is almost worse than clap-trap, I mean

temperate conservatism; the third term does not rest with me to define. The uncommon reader who is interested by these scattered papers may possibly be interested by the small volumes which I have in preparation: *The School of Donne*, *The Outline of Royalism*, and *The Principles of Modern Heresy*.

I wish to acknowledge my obligation to the editors of *The Times Literary Supplement*, *Theology*, *The Dial* (New York), and *The Forum* (New York), in which reviews these essays appeared.

T. S. E.

CONTENTS

———

I.

LANCELOT ANDREWES

THE RIGHT REVEREND FATHER IN GOD, LANCE-
lot Bishop of Winchester, died on September 25,
1626. During his lifetime he enjoyed a distinguished reputation for the excellence of his
sermons, for the conduct of his diocese, for his
ability in controversy displayed against Cardi-
nal Bellarmine, and for the decorum and devotion of his private life. Some years after
Andrewes's death, Lord Clearendon, in his
History of the Rebellion, expressed regret that
Andrewes had not been chosen instead of
Abbott to the Archbishopric of Canterbury, for
thus affairs in England might have taken a
different course. By authorities on the history of
the English Church Andrewes is still accorded
a high, perhaps the highest, place; among persons interested in devotion his "Private Prayers"
are not unknown. But among those persons
who read sermons, if they read them at all, as
specimens of English prose, Andrewes is little
known. His sermons are too well built to be
readily quotable; they stick too closely to the
point to be entertaining. Yet they rank with
the finest English prose of their time, of any
time. Before attempting to remove the remains

[3]

of his reputation to a last resting place in the dreary cemetery of literature, it is desirable to remind the reader of Andrewes's position in history.

The Church of England is the creation not of the reign of Henry VIII or of the reign of Edward VI, but of the reign of Elizabeth. The *via media* which is the spirit of Anglicanism was the spirit of Elizabeth in all things; the last of the humble Welsh family of Tudor was the first and most complete incarnation of English policy. The taste or sensibility of Elizabeth, developed by her intuitive knowledge of the right policy for the hour and her ability to choose the right men to carry out that policy, determined the future of the English Church. In its persistence in finding a mean between Papacy and Presbytery the English Church under Elizabeth became something representative of the finest spirit of England of the time. It came to reflect not only the personality of Elizabeth herself, but the best community of her subjects of every rank. Other religious impulses, of varying degrees of spiritual value, were to assert themselves with greater vehemence during the next two reigns. But the Church at the end of the reign of Elizabeth, and as developed in certain directions under the next reign, was a masterpiece of ecclesiastical statesmanship. The same authority that made use of Gresham, and of Walsingham, and of Cecil, appointed Parker to the Archbishopric of Canterbury; the same authority was later to appoint Whitgift to the same office.

To the ordinary cultivated student of civilization the genesis of a Church is of little interest, and at all events we must not confound the history of a Church with its spiritual meaning. To the ordinary observer the English Church in history means Hooker and Jeremy Taylor —and should mean Andrewes also: it means George Herbert, and it means the churches of Christopher Wren. This is not an error: a Church is to be judged by its intellectual fruits, by its influence on the sensibility of the most sensitive and on the intellect of the most intelligent, and it must be made real to the eye by monuments of artistic merit. The English

[5]

Church has no literary monument equal to that of Dante, no intellectual monument equal to that of St. Thomas, no devotional monument equal to that of St. John of the Cross, no building so beautiful as the Cathedral of Modena or the basilica of St. Zeno in Verona. But there are those for whom the City churches are as precious as any of the four hundred odd churches in Rome which are in no danger of demolition, and for whom St. Paul's, in comparison with St. Peter's, is not lacking in decency; and the English devotional verse of the seventeenth century—admitting the one difficult case of conversion, that of Crashaw—finer than that of any other country or religion at the time.

The intellectual achievement and the prose style of Hooker and Andrewes came to complete the structure of the English Church as the philosophy of the thirteenth century crowns the Catholic Church. To make this statement is not to compare the "Laws of Ecclesiastical Polity" with the "Summa." The seventeenth century was not an age in which the Churches

[6]

occupied themselves with metaphysics, and none of the writings of the fathers of the English Church belongs to the category of speculative philosophy. But the achievement of Hooker and Andrewes was to make the English Church more worthy of intellectual assent. No religion can survive the judgment of history unless the best minds of its time have collaborated in its construction; if the Church of Elizabeth is worthy of the age of Shakespeare and Jonson, that is because of the work of Hooker and Andrewes.

The writings of both Hooker and Andrewes illustrate that determination to stick to essentials, that awareness of the needs of the time, the desire for clarity and precision on matters of importance, and the indifference to matters indifferent, which was the general policy of Elizabeth. These characteristics are illustrated in the definition of the Church in the second book of the "Ecclesiastical Polity." ("The Church of Christ which was from the beginning is and continueth until the end.") And in both Hooker and Andrewes—the latter the friend

and intimate of Isaac Casaubon—we find also
that breadth of culture, an ease with humanism
and Renaissance learning, which helped to
put them on terms of equality with their Continental antagonists and to elevate their church
above the position of a local heretical sect. They
were fathers of a national Church and they
were Europeans. Compare a sermon of Andrewes with a sermon by another earlier master,
Latimer. It is not merely that Andrewes knew
Greek, or that Latimer was addressing a far
less cultivated public, or that the sermons of
Andrewes are peppered with allusion and quotation. It is rather that Latimer, the preacher of
Henry VIII and Edward VI, is merely a
Protestant; but the voice of Andrewes is the
voice of a man who has a formed visible
Church behind him, who speaks with the old
authority and the new culture. It is the difference of negative and positive: Andrewes is the
first great preacher of the English Catholic
Church.

The sermons of Andrewes are not easy reading. They are only for the reader who can ele-

[8]

vate himself to the subject. The most conspicuous qualities of the style are three: ordonnance, or arrangement and structure, precision in the use of words, and relevant intensity. The last remains to be defined. All of them are best elucidated by comparison with a prose which is much more widely known, but to which I believe that we must assign a lower place—that of Donne. Donne's sermons, or fragments from Donne's sermons, are certainly known to hundreds who have hardly heard of Andrewes; and they are known precisely for the reasons because of which they are inferior to those of Andrewes. In the introduction to an admirable selection of passages from Donne's sermons, which was published a few years ago by the Oxford Press, Mr. Logan Pearsall Smith, after "trying to explain Donne's sermons and account for them in a satisfactory manner," observes:

And yet in these, as in his poems, there remains something baffling and enigmatic which still eludes our last analysis. Reading these old hortatory and dogmatic pages, the thought suggests itself that Donne is often saying something else, something poignant and personal, and yet, in the end, in-communicable to us.

We may cavil at the word "incommunicable," and pause to ask whether the incommunicable is not often the vague and unformed; but the statement is essentially right. About Donne there hangs the shadow of the impure motive; and impure motives lend their aid to a facile success. He is a little of the religious spellbinder, the Reverend Billy Sunday of his time, the flesh-creeper, the sorcerer of emotional orgy. We emphasize this aspect to the point of the grotesque. Donne had a trained mind; but without belittling the intensity or the profundity of his experience, we can suggest that this ex-perience was not perfectly controlled, and that he lacked spiritual discipline.

But Bishop Andrewes is one of the community of the born spiritual, one

che in questo mondo,
contemplando, gustò di quella pace.

Intellect and sensibility were in harmony; and hence arise the particular qualities of his style.

Those who would prove this harmony would
do well to examine, before proceeding to the
sermons, the volume of *Preces Privatæ*. This
book, composed by him for his private de-
votions, was printed only after his death; a few
manuscript copies may have been given away
during his lifetime—one bears the name of
William Laud. It appears to have been written
in Latin and translated by him into Greek;
some of it is in Hebrew; it has been several times
translated into English. The most recent edition
is the translation of F. E. Brightman, with an
interesting introduction, in 1903 (Methuen).
They are almost wholly an arrangement of
Biblical texts, and of texts from elsewhere in
Andrewes's immense theological reading. Canon
Brightman has a paragraph of admirable criticism of these prayers which deserves to be
quoted in full:

But the structure is not merely an external
scheme or framework: the internal structure is as
close as the external. Andrewes develops an idea
he has in his mind: every line tells and adds something. He does not expatiate, but moves forward:

if he repeats, it is because the repetition has a real force of expression; if he accumulates, each new word or phrase represents a new development, a substantive addition to what he is saying. He assimilates his material and advances by means of it. His quotation is not decoration or irrelevance, but the matter in which he expresses what he wants to say. His single thoughts are no doubt often suggested by the words he borrows, but the thoughts are made his own, and the constructive force, the fire that fuses them, is his own. And this internal, progressive, often poetic structure is marked outwardly. The editions have not always reproduced this feature of the *Preces*, nor perhaps is it possible in any ordinary page to represent the structure adequately; but in the manuscript the intention is clear enough. The prayers are arranged, not merely in paragraphs, but in lines advanced and recessed, so as in a measure to mark the inner structure and the steps and stages of the movement. Both in form and in matter Andrewes's prayers may often be described rather as hymns.

The first part of this excellent piece of criticism may be applied equally well to the prose of Andrewes's sermons. The prayers themselves, which, as Canon Brightman seems to hint, should take for Anglicans a place beside the

Exercises of St. Ignatius and the works of St. François de Sales, illustrate the devotion to private prayer (Andrewes is said to have passed nearly five hours a day in prayer) and to public ritual which Andrewes bequeathed to William Laud; and his passion for order in religion is reflected in his passion for order in prose.

Readers who hesitate before the five large volumes of Andrewes's sermons in *The Library of Anglo-Catholic Theology* may find their introduction more easy through the *Seventeen Sermons on the Nativity*, which were published separately in a small volume by Griffith, Farran, Okeden and Welsh, in *The Ancient and Modern Library of Theological Literature*, and which can still be picked up here and there. It is an additional advantage that these sermons are all on the same subject, the Incarnation; they are the Christmas Day sermons preached before King James between 1605 and 1624. And in the sermons preached before King James, himself a theologian, Andrewes was not hampered as he sometimes was in addressing more popular

[13]

audiences. His erudition had full play, and his erudition is essential to his originality.

Bishop Andrewes, as was hinted above, tried to confine himself in his sermons to the elucidation of what he considered essential in dogma; he said himself that in sixteen years he had never alluded to the question of predestination, to which the Puritans, following their continental brethren, attached so much importance. The Incarnation was to him an essential dogma, and we are able to compare seventeen developments of the same idea. Reading Andrewes on such a theme is like listening to a great Hellenist expounding a text of the "Posterior Analytics": altering the punctuation, inserting or removing a comma or a semi-colon to make an obscure passage suddenly luminous, dwelling on a single word, comparing its use in its nearer and in its most remote contexts, purifying a disturbed or cryptic lecture-note into lucid profundity. To persons whose minds are habituated to feed on the vague jargon of our time, when we have a vocabulary for everything and exact ideas about nothing—when a word half-understood, torn from its place in some alien or half-formed science, as of psychology, conceals from both writer and reader the utter meaninglessness of a statement, when all dogma is in doubt except the dogmas of sciences of which we have read in the newspapers, when the language of theology itself, under the influence of an undisciplined mysticism of popular philosophy, tends to become a language of tergiversation—Andrewes may seem pedantic and verbal. It is only when we have saturated ourselves in his prose, followed the movement of his thought, that we find his examination of words terminating in the ecstasy of assent. Andrewes takes a word and derives the world from it; squeezing and squeezing the word until it yields a full juice of meaning which we should never have supposed any word to possess. In this process the qualities which we have mentioned, of ordonnance and precision, are exercised.

Take, almost at random, a passage from Andrewes's exposition of the text "That there is born unto you this day a Saviour, Which is

Christ the Lord, in the City of David" (Luke ii, 10, 11). Any passage that we can choose must be torn violently from its context.

Who is it? Three things are said of this Child by the Angel. (1) He is "a Saviour." (2) "Which is Christ." (3) "Christ the Lord." Three of his titles, well and orderly inferred one of another by good consequence. We cannot miss one of them; they be necessary all. Our method on earth is to begin with great; in heaven they begin with good first.

First, then, "a Saviour"; that is His name, Jesus, *Soter;* and in that Name His benefit, *Salus,* "saving health or salvation." Such a name as the great Orator himself saith of it, *Soter, hoc quantum est? Ita magnum est ut latino uno verbo exprimi non possit.* "This name Saviour is so great as no one word can express the force of it."

But we are not so much to regard the *ecce* how great it is, as *gaudium* what joy is in it; that is the point we are to speak to. And for that, men may talk what they will, but sure there is no joy in the world to the joy of a man saved; no joy so great, no news so welcome, as to one ready to perish, in case of a lost man, to hear of one that will save him. In danger of perishing by sickness, to hear of one will make him well again; by sentence of the law, of one with a pardon to save his life; by enemies, of one that will rescue and set him in safety. Tell any of these, assure them but of a Saviour, it is the best news he ever heard in his life. There is joy in the name of a Saviour. And even this way, this Child is a Saviour too. *Potest hoc facere, sed hoc non est opus Ejus.* "This He can do, but this is not His work"; a farther matter there is, a greater salvation He came for. And it may be we need not any of these; we are not presently sick, in no fear of the law, in no danger of enemies. And it may be, if we were, we fancy to ourselves to be relieved some other way. But that which He came for, that saving we need all; and none but He can help us to it. We have therefore all cause to be glad for the Birth of this Saviour.

And then, after this succession of short sentences —no one is more master of the short sentence than Andrewes—in which the effort is to find the exact meaning and make that meaning live, he slightly but sufficiently alters the rhythm in proceeding more at large:

I know not how, but when we hear of saving or mention of a Saviour, presently our mind is carried to the saving of our skin, of our temporal state, of our bodily life, and farther saving we think not of. But there is another life not to be forgotten, and greater the dangers, and the destruction more to be feared than of this here, and it would be well sometimes we were remembered of it. Besides our skin and flesh a soul we have, and it is our better part by far, that also hath need of a Saviour; that hath her destruction out of which, that hath her destroyer from which she would be saved, and those would be thought on. Indeed our chief thought and care would be for that; how to escape the wrath, how to be saved from the destruction to come, whither our sins will certainly bring us. Sin it is will destroy us all.

In this extraordinary prose, which appears to repeat, to stand still, but is nevertheless proceeding in the most deliberate and orderly manner, there are often flashing phrases which never desert the memory. In an age of adventure and experiment in language, Andrewes is one of the most resourceful of authors in his devices for seizing the attention and impressing the memory. Phrases such as "Christ is no wild-cat. What talk ye of twelve days?" or "the word within a word, unable to speak a word," do not desert us; nor do the sentences in which, before extracting all the spiritual meaning of a text, Andrewes forces a concrete presence upon us.

LANCELOT ANDREWES

Of the wise men come from the East:

It was no summer progress. A cold coming they
had of it at this time of the year, just the worst time
of the year to take a journey, and specially a long
journey in. The ways deep, the weather sharp, the
days short, the sun farthest off, *in solstitio brumali*,
"the very dead of winter."

Of "the Word made flesh," again:

I add yet farther; what flesh? The flesh of an
infant. What, *Verbum infans*, the Word an infant?
The Word, and not be able to speak a word? How
evil agreeth this! This He put up. How born, how
entertained? In a stately palace, cradle of ivory,
robes of estate? No; but a stable for His palace, a
manger for His cradle, poor clouts for His array.

He will not hesitate to hammer, to inflect,
even to play upon a word for the sake of driving
home its meaning:

Let us then make this so accepted a time in itself
twice acceptable by our accepting, which He will
acceptably take at our hands.

We can now better estimate what is this that
we have called relevant intensity, for we have
had enough of passages from Andrewes to

recognize the extremity of his difference from Donne.

Everyone knows a passage from a sermon of Donne's, which is given by Mr. Pearsall Smith under the title of "I am Not all Here."

I am here speaking to you, and yet I consider by the way, in the same instant, what it is likely you will say to one another, when I have done, you are not all here neither; you are here now, hearing me, and yet you are thinking that you have heard a better sermon somewhere else of this text before; you are here, and yet you think you could have heard some other doctrine of downright *Predestination* and *Reprobation* roundly delivered somewhere else with more edification to you; you are here, and you remember yourselves that now yee think of it: This had been the fittest time, now, when everybody else is at church, to have made such a private visit; and because you would bee there, you are there,

after which Mr. Pearsall Smith very happily places the paragraph on "Imperfect Prayers":

A memory of yesterday's pleasures, a feare of tomorrow's dangers, a straw under my knee, a noise in mine eare, a light in mine eye, an anything a nothing, a fancy, a Chimera in my braine, troubles me in my prayer. So certainely is there nothing, nothing in spirituall things, perfect in this world. ,

These are thoughts which would never have come to Andrewes. When Andrewes begins his sermon, from beginning to end you are sure that he is wholly in his subject, unaware of anything else, that his emotion grows as he penetrates more deeply into his subject, that he is finally "alone with the Alone," with the mystery which he is seeking to grasp more and more firmly. One is reminded of the words of Arnold about the preaching of Newman. Andrewes's emotion is purely contemplative; it is not personal, it is wholly evoked by the object of contemplation, to which it is adequate; his emotion is wholly contained in and explained by its object. But with Donne there is always the something else, the "baffling" of which Mr. Pearsall Smith speaks in his introduction. Donne is a "personality" in a sense in which Andrewes is not: his sermons, one feels, are a "means of self-expression." He is constantly finding an object which shall be adequate to his feelings; Andrewes is wholly absorbed in the object and therefore responds with the adequate emotion. Andrewes has the *goùt pour la vie spirituelle*, which is not native to Donne. On the other hand, it would be a great mistake to remember only that Donne was called to the priesthood by King James against his will, and that he accepted a benefice because he had no other way of making a living. Donne had a genuine taste both for theology and for religious emotion; but he belonged to that class of persons, of which there are always one or two examples in the modern world, who seek refuge in religion from the tumults of a strong emotional temperament which can find no complete satisfaction elsewhere. He is not wholly without kinship to Huysmans.

But Donne is not the less valuable, though he is the more dangerous for this reason. Of the two men, it may be said that Andrewes is the more medieval, because he is the more pure, and because his bond was with the Church, with tradition. His intellect was satisfied by theology and his sensibility by prayer and liturgy. Donne is the more modern—if we are careful to take this word exactly, without any implication of value, or any suggestion that we must have more sympathy with Donne than with Andrewes. Donne is much less the mystic; he is primarily interested in man. He is much less traditional. In his thought Donne has, on the one hand, much more in common with the Jesuits, and, on the other hand, much more in common with the Calvinists, than has Andrewes. Donne many times betrays the consequences of early Jesuit influence and of his later studies in Jesuit literature; in his cunning knowledge of the weaknesses of the human heart, his understanding of human sin, his skill in coaxing and persuading the attention of the variable human mind to Divine objects, and in a kind of smiling tolerance among his menaces of damnation. He is dangerous only for those who find in his sermons an indulgence of their sensibility, or for those who, fascinated by "personality" in the romantic sense of the word —for those who find in "personality" an ultimate value—forget that in the spiritual hierarchy there are places higher than that of Donne. Donne will certainly have always more readers than Andrewes, for the reason that his sermons can be read in detached passages and for the reason that they can be read by those who have no interest in the subject. He has many means of appeal, and appeals to many temperaments and minds, and, among others, to those capable of a certain wantonness of the spirit. Andrewes will never have many readers in any one generation, and his will never be the immortality of anthologies. Yet his prose is not inferior to that of any sermons in the language, unless it be some of Newman's. And even the larger public which does not read him may do well to remember his greatness in history—a place second to none in the history of the formation of the English Church.

II.

JOHN BRAMHALL

JOHN BRAMHALL, BISHOP OF DERRY UNDER Charles I and Primate of Ireland under Charles II, is not at all an easy subject for a biography. He was a great man; but either by defect of genius or by ill-luck he is not known as he should be known, and his works are not read as they should be read. Indeed, it is largely ill luck. Not only were his immense energy and ability divided among a number of important actions, so that he has never become the symbolical representative of anything; but some of his most important activity was exerted upon causes which are now forgotten. As Bishop of Derry, as the lieutenant of Wentworth and Laud, he did much to reform and establish the Irish Church and to bring it into conformity with the English Church; he saw his work largely undone by Cromwell; as Primate of Ireland during the first years of Charles II, and in his old age, he set to work to build it up again. Had his labours been in England instead of Ireland he might now be better remembered. His middle years were spent in exile; and perhaps it is the work he performed during these years, often in illness, danger, and vicissitudes, that

[27]

should earn him particular gratitude from his Church. This is a chapter of Church history which is too little known; few people realize how near in those times the English Church came to perishing utterly, or realize that had the Commonwealth survived a few years longer the Church would have fallen into a disorder from which it might never have recovered. During the exile Bramhall was the stoutest inheritor of the tradition of Andrewes and Laud.

Dr. Sparrow-Simpson has treated the history of Bramhall's career in Ireland and his activities abroad during the Commonwealth fully, but with a proper sense of proportion.[1] He leaves himself space to devote several chapters to Bramhall's controversial writings; he is specially to be praised for the skill with which he had digested these writings and condensed and organized so much various information into two hundred and fifty-one pages. With the purely historical matter I am not competent to deal; Bramhall's life includes an important part of the

---

[1] *Archbishop Bramhall*. By W. J. Sparrow-Simpson, D.D. (In the English Theologians Series.) S.P.C.K.

history of the Church and the history of England. But there is still much interest to be found in Bramhall's writings, and some of them are very much to the point at the present day. One part of his work that is of particular importance is his controversy with Hobbes. It is sometimes cited by historians of philosophy, but has never received the attention it deserves. Bramhall, as Dr. Sparrow-Simpson points out, had by no means the worst of the argument, and the whole debate, with the two striking and opposed personalities engaged in it, throws light upon the condition of philosophy and theology at that time. The most important of the questions of issue are two: the freedom of the will and the relation between Church and State.

Thomas Hobbes was one of those extraordinary little upstarts whom the chaotic motions of the Renaissance tossed into an eminence which they hardly deserved and have never lost. When I say the Renaissance I mean for this purpose the period between the decay of scholastic philosophy and the rise of modern science. The thirteenth century had the gift of philosophy, or reason; the later seventeenth century had the gift of mathematics, or science; but the period between had ceased to be rational without having learned to be scientific. There was nothing particularly new about the determinism of Hobbes; but he gave to his determinism and theory of sense perception a new point and piquancy by applying it, so to speak, almost to topical questions; and by his metaphor of Leviathan he provided an ingenious framework on which there was some peg or other to hang every question of philosophy, psychology, government, and economics.

Hobbes shows considerable ingenuity and determination in his attempt to carry out his theory of the Will rigorously to explain the whole and every aspect of human behaviour. It is certain that in the end he lands himself in sophistries. But at the time of Hobbes and Bramhall, and indeed ever since until recently, it was impossible that a controversy on this subject should keep to the point. For a philosopher like Hobbes has already a mixed attitude, partly philosophic and partly scientific; the further degree; just as Hobbes's Theory of Will removes freedom from the individual considered as the object of psychology, but really implies the reality of freewill in society. It will be remembered that Hobbes wished to maintain the activity of human legislation in his deterministic universe; so he considered that law acts as a deterrent force. He did not consider that if human laws themselves are created by the same necessity under which human beings act when encouraged or deterred by the laws, then the whole system ceases to have any meaning, and all values, including his own value of good government, disappear.

It is not to be expected that the arguments advanced by Bramhall against this position should appear very powerful when opposed to the reasonings of modern disciples of Hobbes. But in their own time and place they were excellent. I disregard that part of Bramhall's reasoning which consists in showing that Hobbes's system was incompatible with Christianity. Hobbes was here in a very weak position of which the Bishop with praiseworthy slyness took full advantage. Hobbes was undoubtedly an atheist and could hardly have been unconscious of the fact; but he was no Spinoza, and would hardly have been willing to sacrifice his worldly prospects for the sake of establishing consistency in his argument. Therefore he has always the worst of the debate. But this is a minor point. Bramhall was able to meet Hobbes also on his own ground. His method of attack illustrates very clearly his type of mind. It was not a subtle mind: it had not the refinement necessary to make a scholastic metaphysician, nor was it the mind of a doctor of the Church who could develop and explicate the meaning of a dogma. It was essentially common sense and right instinct, a mind not gifted to discover truth but tenacious to hold it. It was typical of the best theological minds of that age. Hobbes suffers from not only a tactical but a real disadvantage in his confusion of the spheres of psychology and ethics. Bramhall is single-minded; he does not penetrate the real philosophical incoherence of Hobbes's position; but he touches the point of practical importance and implies the profounder objection to Hobbes when he says simply that Hobbes makes praise and blame meaningless. "If a man be born blind or with one eye, we do not blame him for it; but if a man have lost his sight by his intemperance, we blame him justly." This objection is finally unanswerable.

I have asserted that Hobbes's psychological analysis of the human mind has no rational connection with his theory of the State. But it has, of course, an emotional connection; one can say that both doctrines belong naturally to the same temperament. Materialistic determinism and absolutist government fit into the same scheme of life. And this theory of the State shows the same lack of balance which is a general characteristic of philosophers after the Renaissance. Hobbes merely exaggerates one aspect of the good State. In doing so he developed a particularly lamentable theory of the relation between Church and State.

There is no question to which a man like Hobbes can give a less satisfactory answer than that of Church and State. For Hobbes thought in extremes, and in this problem the extreme is always wrong. In the relation of Church and State, a doctrine when pushed to the extreme may even be transformed to the opposite of itself. Hobbes has something in common with Suarez.

Bramhall's position on this subject is characteristic of his sense of realities and his ability to grasp what was expedient. He had also what Hobbes lacked, the historical sense, which is a gift not only of the historian, but of the efficient lawyer, statesman, or theologian. His account of the relations of the English kings with the Papacy, from the earliest times, and his selection of parallels from the history of continental Europe, show both wide knowledge and great skill in argument. His thinking is a perfect example of the pursuit of the *via media*, and the *via media* is of all ways the most difficult to follow. It requires discipline and self-control, it requires both imagination and hold on reality. In a period of debility like our own, few men have the energy to follow the middle way in government; for lazy or tired minds there is only extremity or apathy: dictatorship or communism, with enthusiasm or with indifference. An able Conservative writer, Mr. Keith Feiling, in his *England under the Tudors and Stewarts*, refers to Hobbes as "the acutest thinker of the age." It would be equally true to say that he is the most eminent example in his age of a particularly lazy type of thinker. At any rate, the age owes a very great part of its distinction, both in England and in France, to thinkers of wholly the opposite type to Hobbes.

The French Church in the time of Louis XIV ("*il fut gallicain, ce siècle, et janseniste*") resembled the English Church under the Stuarts in several respects. In both countries a strong and autocratic civil Government controlled and worked with a strongly national Church. In each country there was a certain balance of power; in France between the throne and the papacy; in England an internal balance of power between strong personalities. There was much in common between Bramhall and Bossuet. But between Bramhall and Hobbes there is no sympathy whatever. Superficially their theories of the kingship bear some resemblance to each other. Both men were violently hostile to democracy in any form or degree. Both men believed that the monarch should have absolute power. Bramhall affirmed the divine right of kings: Hobbes rejected this noble faith, and asserted in effect the divine right of power, however come by. But Bramhall's view is not so absurdly romantic, or Hobbes's so soundly reasonable, as might seem. To Bramhall the king himself was a kind of symbol, and his assertion of divine right was a way of laying upon the king a double responsibility. It meant that the king had not merely a civil but a religious obligation toward his people. And the kingship of Bramhall is less absolute than the kingship of Hobbes. For Hobbes the Church was merely a department of the State, to be run exactly as the king thought best. Bramhall does not tell us clearly what would be the duties of a private citizen if the king should violate or overturn the Christian religion, but he obviously leaves a wide expedient margin for resistance or justified rebellion. It is curious that the system of

JOHN BRAMHALL

Hobbes, as Dr. Sparrow-Simpson has observed, not only insists on autocracy but tolerates *unjustified* revolution. Hobbes's theory is in some ways very near to that of Machiavelli, with this important exception, that he has none of Machiavelli's profound observation and none of Machiavelli's limiting wisdom. The sole test and justification for Hobbes is in the end merely material success. For Hobbes all standards of good and evil are frankly relative.

It is extraordinary that a philosophy so essentially revolutionary as that of Hobbes, and so similar to that of contemporary Russia, should ever have been supposed to give any support to Toryism. But its ambiguity is largely responsible for its success. Hobbes was a revolutionary in thought and a timid conservative in action; and his theory of government is congenial to that type of person who is conservative from prudence but revolutionary in his dreams. This type of person is not altogether uncommon. In Hobbes there are symptoms of the same mentality as Nietzsche: his belief in violence is a confession of weakness. Hobbes's violence is of a type that often appeals to gentle people. His specious effect of unity between a very simple theory of sense perception and an equally simple theory of government is of a kind that will always be popular because it appears to be intellectual but is really emotional, and therefore very soothing to lazy minds.

Bramhall's abilities of thought and language are nowhere better displayed than in his *Just Vindication of the English Church*. As for the language of Bramhall, I think that Dr. Sparrow-Simpson does him less than justice. It is true that he employs in his vocabulary the most extraordinary confections of Latinity, but the catalogue of some of these expressions which Dr. Sparrow-Simpson gives would lead one to believe that they occur in every sentence. And although Bramhall is not an easy writer, his phrases are lucid and direct and occasionally have real beauty and rhythm. A theologian of his powers, at that period of English prose, a man trained on the theology and the style of

[40]

Bishop Andrewes, could hardly fail to write prose of distinction.

Every sudden passionate heat or misunderstanding or shaking of charity amongst Christians, though it were even between the principal pastors of the Church, is not presently schism. As that between Saint Paul and Barnabas in the Acts of the Apostles—who dare say that either of them were schismatic? or that between Saint Hierome and Ruffinus, who charged one another mutually with heresy; or that between Saint Chrysostom and Epiphanius, who refused to join in prayers; Saint Chrysostom wishing that Epiphanius might never return home alive, and Epiphanius wishing that Saint Chrysostom might not die a Bishop; both which things, by the just disposition of Almighty God, fell out according to the passionate and uncharitable desires of these holy persons; who had Christian charity still radicated in their hearts, though the violent torrent of sudden passion did for a time beat down all other respects before it.

This is rather heavy going, and the word "radicated" is one of those blemishes to which Dr. Sparrow-Simpson calls attention; but the style has distinction. In prose style, as well as in theology, Bramhall is a link between the generation of Andrewes and the generation of Jeremy Taylor. The prose of Bramhall is great prose only in the sense that it is good prose of a great epoch. I cannot believe that Bramhall was a great preacher. Andrewes and Donne and Taylor had a poetic sensibility; that is to say, they had the sensitiveness necessary to record and to bring to convergence on a theological point a multitude of fleeting but universal feeling. Their words linger and echo in the mind as Bramhall's never do; we forget Bramhall's phrases the moment we turn away from Bramhall's subject.

But for *ordonnance*, logical arrangement, for mastery of every fact relevant to a thesis, Bramhall is surpassed only by Hooker; and I am not sure that in the structure of the *Just Vindication of the English Church* he does not surpass even Hooker. And this book is no antiquity; it is a work which ought to be studied by anyone to whom the relation of Church and State is an actual and importunate problem. There could hardly be a greater difference than that between the situation during the first half of the

[42]

seventeenth century and the situation to-day.
Yet the differences are such as to make the work
of Bramhall the more pertinent to our problems.
For they are differences in relation to a fundamental unity of thought between Bramhall, and
what he represents, and ourselves.

III.

NICCOLO MACHIAVELLI

"BECAUSE THIS IS TO BE ASSERTED IN GENERAL of men, that they are ungrateful, fickle, false, cowards, covetous, and as long as you succeed they are yours entirely." This sentence, and similar sentences torn from their context, have rankled and worried the minds of men for four hundred years: the words of a retired, inoffensive, quiet Florentine patriot occupied in chopping trees and conversing with peasants on his meagre estate. Machiavelli has been the torment of Jesuits and Calvinists, the idol of Napoleons and Nietzsches, a stock figure for Elizabethan drama, and the exampler of a Mussolini or a Lenin. Machiavelli has been called a cynic; but there could be no stronger inspiration to "cynicism" than the history of Machiavelli's reputation. No history could illustrate better than that of the reputation of Machiavelli the triviality and the irrelevance of influence. His message has been falsified by persistent romanticism ever since his death. To the humbug of every century Machiavelli has contributed. And yet no great man has been so completely misunderstood. He is always placed a little askew. He does not belong with

Aristotle, or with Dante, in political theory; he attempted something different. He does not belong with Napoleon, and still less with Nietzsche. His statements lend themselves to any modern theory of the State, but they belong with none.

On the occasion of Niccolo Machiavelli's anniversary, we should concern ourselves not so much with the history of his influence—which is merely the history of the various ways in which he has been misunderstood—as with the nature of his thought and the reasons why it should have had such influence.

"So that in the first place I put for a general inclination of all mankind a perpetual and restless desire of power after power, that ceaseth only in death." Such words of Hobbes seem at first to be uttered in the same tone as those quoted from Machiavelli; and the two names have often been brought together; but the spirit and purpose of Hobbes and of Machiavelli are wholly different. *The Prince* is often taken in the same sense as *Leviathan*. But Machiavelli is not only not a philosopher of

politics in the sense of Aristotle and Dante, he is
still less a philosopher in the sense of Hobbes.
He has the lucidity of Aristotle and the patriot-
ism of Dante, but with Hobbes he has little in
common. Machiavelli is wholly *devoted*—to his
task of his own place and time; yet by surrender-
ing himself to the cause of his particular State,
and to the greater cause of the united Italy
which he desired, he arrives at a far greater
impersonality and detachment than Hobbes.
Hobbes is not passionately moved by the
spectacle of national disaster; he is interested
in his own theory; and we can see his theory as
partly an outcome of the weaknesses and distortions of his own temperament. In the statements of Hobbes about human nature there is
often an over-emphasis, a touch of spleen arising
probably from some perception of the weakness
and failure of his own life and character. This
over-emphasis, so common in a certain type of
philosopher since Hobbes's time, may be rightly
associated with cynicism. For true cynicism is a
fault of the temperament of the observer, not a
conclusion arising naturally out of the con-

[49]

templation of the object; it is quite the reverse of "facing facts." In Machiavelli there is no cynicism whatever. No spot of the weaknesses and failures of his own life and character mars the clear glass of his vision. In detail, no doubt, where the meanings of words suffer a slight alteration, we feel a conscious irony; but his total view was unimpaired by any such emotional colour. Such a view of life as Machiavelli's implies a state of the soul which may be called a state of innocence. A view like Hobbes's is slightly theatrical and almost sentimental. The impersonality and innocence of Machiavelli is so rare that it may well be the clue to both his perpetual influence over men and the perpetual distortion which he suffers in the minds of men less pure than himself.

We do not mean that Machiavelli is wholly cold and impassive. On the contrary, he provides one more piece of evidence that great intellectual power arises from great passions. Machiavelli was not only a patriot, but his patriotic passion is the motor of his mind. It is all very well for writers like Lord Morley to present Machiavelli as a stealthy inhuman surgeon, indifferent to moral exhortation and caring only for his clinical examination. Lord Morley had not, like Machiavelli, seen his country torn and ravaged, humiliated not only by foreign invaders, but by foreign invaders brought in by factious native princes. The humiliation of Italy was to Machiavelli a personal humiliation, and the origin of his thought and his writing.

This intense nationalism by no means suppressed or distorted in Machiavelli the other moral or spiritual values. Only, he is in his writings occupied with these from one point of view always, occupied with them always in their relation to the State. His conception of the State is a large and generous one. He is the adviser of the Prince only because he cares passionately for the good of the commonwealth. For a man like Napoleon—who himself spoke highly of Machiavelli, and whose sense of reality made Machiavelli very sympathetic to him—Machiavelli could have felt only aversion; a foreign usurper and a violent egotist Napoleon would have seemed to him. And Machiavelli is not interested in the modern idea of Empire; a united Italy was the limit of his vision; and indeed we often feel, in reading the most important of his works, the *Discourses on the Decades of Livy*, that he has far more admiration for Republican Rome than for Imperial Rome. His first thought always is for peace and prosperity and the happiness of the governed; but he knows quite well that this happiness does not reside merely in peace and wealth. It depends upon, and in turn supports. the *virtue* of the citizens. Civic virtue cannot exist without a measure of liberty, and he is constantly concerned with what relative liberty is obtainable.

It seldom happens that the demands of a free people are either unreasonable or prejudicial to liberty, as they commonly proceed either from actual oppression, or the dread of it; but if that apprehension should prove groundless, it is no difficult matter to pacify them by a public conference, where they are always ready to listen to any man of worth and authority that shall think fit to harangue them: for though the people may sometimes be in an error, as Tully says, they are open to better information, and soon convinced, when a person of whose veracity and integrity they have a good opinion undertakes to show them their mistake.

Machiavelli's attitude toward religion and toward the religion of his country has often been the object of misunderstanding. His attitude is that of a statesman, and is as noble as that of any statesman, *qua* statesman. In fact, it could be no other than it is. He is opposed neither to religion nor to the Catholic Church. He saw quite clearly, as he could hardly have avoided seeing, the corruption of the Church and the baseness of the eminent ecclesiastics with whom he had to do. And in the *Mandragora*, his brilliant comedy, he makes excellent fun of the more petty corruptions of the priesthood. He saw, on the one hand, the extent to which the Church and the powerful individual nobles of the Church had contributed to the dissension and desolation of his country. But he maintained steadily that an established Church was of the greatest value to a State.

[53]

All these things being considered, I conclude, that the introduction of Religion at Rome by Numa was one of the causes that chiefly contributed to its grandeur and felicity: for Religion produced good order, and good order is generally attended with good fortune and success in any undertaking. And, as a strict observance of Divine worship and religious duties always tends to the aggrandizement of a State, so a neglect and contempt of them may be reckoned amongst the first causes of its ruin. For, where there is no fear of God, it must either fall to destruction, or be supported by the reverence shown to a good Prince; which indeed may sustain it for a while, and supply the want of Religion in his Subjects. But as human life is short, the Government must of course sink into decay when the virtue that upheld and informed it is extinct.

And later (in the Discourses) he says still more positively, in words which Archbishop Laud would have approved:

The rulers of all States, whether Kingdoms or Commonwealths, who would preserve their governments firm and entire, ought above all things to take care that Religion is held in the highest veneration, and its ceremonies at all times uncorrupted and inviolable; for there is no surer prognostic of impending ruin in any State, than to see **Divine** worship neglected or despised.

And he goes on to show, in the same chapter, how the neglect of religion, occasioned by the vagaries of the Church of Rome, had contributed to the ruin of Italy. It is quite possible that an established National Church, such as the Church of England, might have seemed to Machiavelli the best establishment for a Christian commonwealth; but that a religious establishment of some kind is necessary to a nation he is quite sure. If his words were true then they are true now. As for Machiavelli's "personal" religion, it seems to have been as genuine and sincere as that of any man who is not a specialist in devotion but intensely a specialist in statesmanship; and he died with the ministrations of a priest about him. He saw quite clearly and knew instinctively that the efforts of a man like Savonarola could bring no good; his real objection was not to the spirit of Savonarola so much as to the contradiction between the methods of **Savonarola** and good statesmanship. But with a destructive mind like that of Voltaire the essentially constructive mind of Machiavelli could have felt no community.

In several chapters of *The Prince* and in the *Art of War* it is quite clear that in considering warfare Machiavelli is concerned always with the positive and the constructive. In warfare, and in military government and occupation, he is interested as much in the moral forces as in the technical devices. In his remarks on colonization, on the manner of occupying a foreign territory, and in his repeated admonitions against the use of mercenary troops he is always holding up for admiration the patriot prince and the patriot citizenry. For the prince who is merely a general he has little patience; of an empire like that of Napoleon he would have said at the outset that it could not last. You cannot govern people for ever against their will; and some foreign peoples you cannot rule at all; but if you have to govern an alien and inferior people—a people inferior in the art of government—then you must use every means to make them contented and to persuade them that your government is to their interest. Liberty is good; but more important is order; and the maintenance of order justifies every means. But his soldiers should be citizen soldiers, fighting for something really valuable; and the prince must be a statesman always, and a warrior only when necessary.

No account of Machiavelli's views can be more than fragmentary. For though he is constructive he is not a system builder; and his thoughts can be repeated but not summarized. It is perhaps a character of his amazing exactness of vision and statement that he should have no "system"; for a system almost inevitably requires slight distortions and omissions, and Machiavelli would distort and omit nothing. But what is more curious is that no account of recapitulation of his thought seems to give any clue either to his greatness or to his great and grotesque reputation. When we first read him we receive the impression neither of a great soul nor of a dæmoniac intellect; but merely of a modest and honest observer setting down matters of fact and comments so true as to be platitudinous. Only after slow absorption and the repeated contrasts which strike the mind between such honesty and the common deceptions, dishonesties, and tergiversations of the human mind in general does his unique greatness reach us. We do not imply that Machiavelli's thought is a solitary exception. A French writer, M. Charles Benoist, has devoted a volume to *Le machiavélisme avant Machiavel*. There are parallels in his own time. Machiavelli could hardly have known Commynes, but the mind and the vision of the great Belgian diplomat who served Louis of France so long and so well are closely akin to those of Machiavelli. But Machiavelli, apart from his difference of method, is a far purer and more intense spirit.

The passionate nationalism of Machiavelli was hardly likely to be understood in his own time; least of all by his compatriots. But the honesty of his mind is such as is hardly understood at any time. From the first his writings seem to have fascinated and terrified Europe. From the fascination people could not escape;

[58]

from the terror they escaped by turning him into a myth of terror. Even in Italy, as Charbonnel shows in *La pensée italienne au XVI siècle*, his thought was immediately distorted. Popes and princes seem to have taken from his books what they wanted, but not what Machiavelli wanted to convey. But as his work penetrated farther abroad the greater became the distortion. In France, and especially among the Huguenots, it aroused the most violent rejoinders. He was treated as hardly more than a clever sycophant giving tips to tyrants on the best ways of oppressing their subjects. In France not only religious partisans but the *politiques*—notably Jean Bodin—fell foul of him. Bodin could not get over Machiavelli's praise of Cæsar Borgia in *The Prince;* although, to anyone who reads the book without prejudice, it should be quite clear in what respects and with what reservations Machiavelli bestows his praise. In England Thomas Cromwell and others admired his work, though it is quite unlikely that they understood him better. But the general impression of Machiavelli in England was due to French influence, to the translation of the *Contre-Machiavel* of Gentillet. At every remove Machiavelli suffered. The civilization of France was in some respects below that of Italy, and the civilization of England had certainly not caught up with the civilization of France. You have only to compare the development of prose style in the three languages. Machiavelli is a master of prose style of any age; his prose is *mature*. There is nothing comparable in France until Montaigne, and Montaigne is not a *classique* for French criticism. And there is nothing comparable in England till Hobbes and Clarendon. But by that time, when the civilization of the three countries was much on a level, there is some deterioration everywhere. Montaigne is inferior to Machiavelli, and Hobbes is inferior to Montaigne. The dramatization of Machiavelli in England had been catalogued by Edward Meyer in his *Machiavelli and the Elizabethan Drama*, and recently discussed more philosophically by Mr. Wyndham Lewis in his extremely interesting study of Shakespeare, *The Lion and the Fox*.

[60]

The figure of Richard III is the testimony of the impression made by Machiavelli, and the falsity of this impression.

We have therefore to inquire what there is about Machiavelli to impress the mind of Europe so prodigiously and so curiously, and why the European mind felt it necessary to deform his doctrine so absurdly. There are certainly contributing causes. The reputation of Italy as the home of fantastic, wanton and diabolical crime filled the French, and still more the English, imagination as they are now filled by the glories of Chicago or Los Angeles, and predisposed imagination toward the creation of a mythical representative for this criminality. But still more the growth of Protestantism—and France, as well as England, was then largely a Protestant country—created a disposition against a man who accepted in his own fashion the orthodox view of original sin. Calvin, whose view of humanity was far more extreme, and certainly more false, than that of Machiavelli, was never treated to such opprobrium; but when the inevitable

[61]

reaction against Calvinism came out of Calvinism, and from Geneva, in the doctrine of
Rousseau, that, too, was hostile to Machiavelli.
For Machiavelli is a doctor of the mean, and the
mean is always insupportable to partisans of the
extreme. A fanatic can be tolerated. The failure
of a fanaticism such as Savonarola's ensures its
toleration by posterity, and even approving
patronage. But Machiavelli was no fanatic; he
merely told the truth about humanity. The
world of human motives which he depicts is
true—that is to say, it is humanity without the
addition of superhuman Grace. It is therefore
tolerable only to persons who have also a definite religious belief; to the effort of the last
three centuries to supply religious belief by
belief in Humanity the creed of Machiavelli
is insupportable. Lord Morley voices the
usual modern hostile admiration of Machiavelli
when he intimates that Machiavelli saw very
clearly what he did see, but that he saw only
half of the truth about human nature. What
Machiavelli did not see about human nature
is the myth of human goodness which for

liberal thought replaces the belief in Divine Grace.

It is easy to admire Machiavelli in a sentimental way. It is only one of the sentimental and histrionic poses of human nature—and human nature is incorrigibly histrionic—to pose as a "realist," a person of "no nonsense," to admire the "brutal frankness" or the "cynicism" of Machiavelli. This is a form of self-satisfaction and self-deception, which merely propagates the Jew of Malta-Nietzsche myth of Machiavelli. In Elizabethan England the reputation of Machiavelli was merely manipulated unconsciously to feed the perpetually recurring tendency to Manichæan heresy: the desire for a devil to worship. The heretical impulses remain fairly constant; they recur in the Satan of Milton and the Cain of Byron. But with these indulgences of human frailties Machiavelli has no traffic. He had none of the instinct to pose; and therefore human beings, in order to accept him at all, had to make him into a dramatic figure. His reputation is the history of the attempt of humanity to protect itself, by secreting a coating of falsehood, against any statement of the truth.

It has been said, in a tone of reproach, that Machiavelli makes no attempt "to persuade." Certainly he was no prophet. For he was concerned first of all with truth, not with persuasion, which is one reason why his prose is great prose, not only of Italian but a model of style for any language. He is a partial Aristotle of politics. But he is partial not because his vision is distorted or his judgment biased, or because of any lack of moral interest, but because of his sole passion for the unity, peace, and prosperity of his country. What makes him a great writer, and for ever a solitary figure, is the purity and single-mindedness of his passion. No one was ever less "Machiavellian" than Machiavelli. Only the pure in heart can blow the gaff on human nature as Machiavelli has done. The cynic can never do it; for the cynic is always impure and sentimental. But it is easy to understand why Machiavelli was not himself a successful politician. For one thing, he had no capacity for self-deception or self-dramatization. The recipe *dors ton sommeil de brute* is applied in many forms, of which Calvin and Rousseau give two variations; but the utility of Machiavelli is his perpetual summons to examination of the weakness and impurity of the soul. We are not likely to forget his political lessons, but his examination of conscience may be too easily overlooked.

IV.

FRANCIS HERBERT BRADLEY

It is unusual that a book so famous and so influential should remain out of print so long as Bradley's *Ethical Studies*.[1] The one edition appeared in 1876: Bradley's refusal to reprint it never wavered. In 1893, in a footnote in *Appearance and Reality*, and in words characteristic of the man, he wrote: "I feel that the appearance of other books, as well as the decay of those superstitions against which largely it was directed, has left me free to consult my own pleasure in the matter." The dates of his three books, the *Ethical Studies* in 1876, the *Principles of Logic* in 1883, and *Appearance and Reality* in 1893, leave us in no doubt that his pleasure was the singular one of thinking rather than the common one of writing books. And Bradley always assumed, with what will remain for those who did not know him a curious blend of humility and irony, an attitude of extreme diffidence about his own work. His *Ethical Studies*, he told us (or told our fathers), did not aim at "the construction of a system of Moral Philosophy." The first words of the preface to

[1] *Ethical Studies*. By F. H. Bradley, O.M., LL.D. Second Edition. (Oxford: Clarendon Press. London: Milford.)

his *Principles of Logic* are: "The following work makes no claim to supply any systematic treatment of logic." He begins the preface to *Appearance and Reality* with the words: "I have described the following work as an essay in metaphysics. Neither in form nor extent does it carry out the idea of a system." The phrase for each book is almost the same. And many readers having in mind Bradley's polemical irony and his obvious zest in using it, his habit of discomfiting an opponent with a sudden profession of ignorance, of inability to understand, or of incapacity for abstruse thought, have concluded that this is all a mere pose—and even a somewhat unscrupulous one. But deeper study of Bradley's mind convinces us that the modesty is real, and his irony the weapon of a modest and highly sensitive man. Indeed, if this had been a pose it would never have worn so well as it has. We have to consider, then, what is the nature of Bradley's influence and why his writings and his personality fascinate those whom they do fascinate; and what are his claims to permanence.

FRANCIS HERBERT BRADLEY

Certainly one of the reasons for the power he still exerts, as well as an indubitable claim to permanence, is his great gift of style. It is for his purposes—and his purposes are more varied than is usually supposed—a perfect style. Its perfection has prevented it from cutting any great figure in prose anthologies and literature manuals, for it is perfectly welded with the matter. Ruskin's works are extremely readable in snippets even for many who take not a particle of interest in the things in which Ruskin was so passionately interested. Hence he survives in anthologies, while his books have fallen into undue neglect. Bradley's books can never fall into this neglect because they will never rise to this notoriety; they come to the hands only of those who are qualified to treat them with respect. But perhaps a profounder difference between a style like Bradley's and a style like Ruskin's is a greater purity and concentration of purpose. One feels that the emotional intensity of Ruskin is partly a deflection of something that was baffled in life, whereas Bradley, like Newman, is directly and wholly that which he is. For the secret of Bradley's style, like that of Bergson—whom he resembles in this if in nothing else—is the intense addiction to an intellectual passion.

The nearest resemblance in style, however, is not Ruskin but Matthew Arnold. It has not been sufficiently observed that Bradley makes use of the same means as Arnold, and for similar ends. To take first the most patent resemblance, we find in Bradley the same type of fun as that which Arnold has with his young friend Arminius. In *The Principles of Logic* there is a celebrated passage in which Bradley is attacking the theory of association of ideas according to Professor Bain, and explains how on this principle an infant comes to recognize a lump of sugar:

A young child, or one of the lower animals, is given on Monday a round piece of sugar, eats it and finds it sweet. On Tuesday it sees a square piece of sugar, and proceeds to eat it. . . . Tuesday's sensation and Monday's image are not only separate facts, which, because alike, are therefore *not* the same; but they differ perceptibly both in quality

[72]

and environment. What is to lead the mind to take one for the other?

Sudden at this crisis, and in pity at distress, there leaves the heaven with rapid wing a goddess Primitive Credulity. Breathing in the ear of the bewildered infant she whispers, The thing which has happened once will happen once more. Sugar was sweet, and sugar will be sweet. And Primitive Credulity is accepted forthwith as the mistress of our life. She leads our steps on the path of experience, until her fallacies, which cannot always be pleasant, at length become suspect. We wake up indignant at the kindly fraud by which the goddess so long has deceived us. So she shakes her wings, and flying to the stars, where there are no philosophers, leaves us here to the guidance of—I cannot think what.

This sort of solemn banter is exactly what an admirer of Arnold is ready to enjoy. But it is not only in his fun, or in his middle style, that Bradley is like Arnold; they are alike in their purple passages. The two following may be compared. By Arnold:

And yet, steeped in sentiment as she lies, spreading her gardens to the moonlight, and whispering from her towers the last enchantments of the Middle

Age, who will deny that Oxford, by her ineffable charm, keeps ever calling us nearer to the true goal of all of us, to the ideal, to perfection—to beauty, in a word, which is only truth seen from another side—nearer, perhaps, than all the science of Tübingen. Adorable dreamer, whose heart has been so romantic! who hast given thyself so prodigally, given thyself to sides and to heroes not mine, only never to the Philistines! home of lost causes, and forsaken beliefs, and unpopular names, and impossible loyalties! what example could ever so inspire us to keep down the Philistine in ourselves, what teacher could ever so save us from that bondage to which we are all prone, that bondage which Goethe, in his incomparable lines on the death of Schiller, makes it his friend's highest praise (and nobly did Schiller deserve the praise) to have left miles out of sight behind him—the bondage of "was uns alle bändigt, *das Gemeine !*"

The passage from *The Principle of Logic* is not so well known:

It may come from a failure in my metaphysics, or from a weakness of the flesh which continues to blind me, but the notion that existence could be the same as understanding strikes as cold and ghost-like as the dreariest materialism. That the glory of this world in the end is appearance leaves the world more glorious, if we feel it is a show of

[74]

some fuller splendour; but the sensuous curtain is a deception and a cheat, if it hides some colourless movement of atoms, some spectral woof of impalpable abstractions, or unearthly ballet of bloodless categories. Though dragged to such conclusions we cannot embrace them. Our principles may be true, but they are not reality. They no more *make* that Whole which commands our devotion than some shredded dissection of human tatters *is* that warm and breathing beauty of flesh which our hearts found delightful.

Any one who is at all sensitive to style will recognize the similarity of tone and tension and beat. It is not altogether certain that the passage from Bradley is not the better; at any rate such a phrase as Arnold's "ineffable charm" has not worn at all well.

But if the two men fought with the same weapons—and fundamentally, in spite of Bradley's assault upon Arnold, for the same causes —the weapons of Bradley had behind them a heavier force and a closer precision. Exactly what Bradley fought for and exactly what he fought against have not been quite understood; understanding has been obscured by the dust of

Bradley's logical battles. People are inclined to believe that what Bradley did was to demolish the logic of Mill and the psychology of Bain. If he had done that, it would have been a lesser service than what he has done; and if he had done that it would have been less of a service than people think, for there is much that is good in the logic of Mill and the psychology of Bain. But Bradley did not attempt to destroy Mill's logic. Any one who reads his own *Principles* will see that his force is directed not against Mill's logic as a whole but only against certain limitations, imperfections and abuses. He left the structure of Mill's logic standing, and never meant to do anything else. On the other hand, the *Ethical Studies* are not merely a demolition of the Utilitarian theory of conduct but an attack upon the whole Utilitarian mind. For Utilitarianism was, as every reader of Arnold knows, a great temple in Philistia. And of this temple Arnold hacked at the ornaments and cast down the images, and his best phrases remain for ever gibing and scolding in our memory. But Bradley, in his

philosophical critique of Utilitarianism, under-
mined the foundations. The spiritual descend-
ants of Bentham have built anew, as they always will; but at least, in building another
temple for the same worship, they have had to
apply a different style of architecture. And this
is the social basis of Bradley's distinction, and
the social basis is even more his claim to our
gratitude than the logical basis: he replaced a
philosophy which was crude and raw and
provincial by one which was, in comparison,
catholic, civilized, and universal. True, he was
influenced by Kant and Hegel and Lotze. But
Kant and Hegel and Lotze are not so despic-
able as some enthusiastic medievalists would
have us believe, and they are, in comparison
with the school of Bentham, catholic and civilized and universal. In fighting the battles that
he fought in the 'seventies and 'eighties Bradley was fighting for a European and ripened and
wise philosophy, against an insular and imma-
ture and cranky one; the same battle that
Arnold was fighting against the *British Banner*,
Judge Edmonds, Newman Weeks, Deborah

Butler, Elderess Polly, Brother Noyes, **Mr.** Murphy, the Licensed Victuallers and the Commercial Travellers.

It is not to say that Arnold's work was vain if we say that it is to be done again; for we must know in advance, if we are prepared for that conflict, that the combat may have truces but never a peace. If we take the widest and wisest view of a Cause, there is no such thing as a Lost Cause because there is no such thing as a Gained Cause. We fight for lost causes because we know that our defeat and dismay may be the preface to our successors' victory, though that victory itself will be temporary; we fight rather to keep something alive than in the expectation that anything will triumph. If Bradley's philosophy is to-day a little out of fashion, we must remark that what has superseded it, what is now in favour, is, for the most part, crude and raw and provincial (though infinitely more technical and scientific) and must perish in its turn. Arnold turned from mid-century Radicalism with the reflection "A new power has suddenly appeared." There is always a new power; but the new power destined to supersede the philosophy which has superseded Bradley will probably be something at the same time older, more patient, more supple and more wise. The chief characteristics of much contemporary philosophy are newness and crudeness, impatience, inflexibility in one respect and fluidity in another, and irresponsibility and lack of wisdom. Of wisdom Bradley had a large share; wisdom consists largely of scepticism and uncynical disillusion; and of these Bradley had a large share. And scepticism and disillusion are a useful equipment for religious understanding; and of that Bradley had a share too.

Those who have read the *Ethical Studies* will be ready with the remark that it was Bradley, in this book and in the year 1876, who knocked the bottom out of *Literature and Dogma*. But that does not mean that the two men were not on the same side; it means only that *Literature and Dogma* is irrelevant to Arnold's main position as given in the Essays and in *Culture and Anarchy*, that the greatest weakness of Arnold's culture was his weakness in philosophical training, and that in philosophical criticism Bradley exhibits the same type of culture that Arnold exhibited in political and social criticism. Arnold had made an excursion into a field for which he was not armed. Bradley's attack upon Arnold does not take up much space, but Bradley was economical of words; it is all in a few paragraphs and a few footnotes to the "Concluding Remarks":

But here once more "culture" has come to our aid, and has shown us how here, as everywhere, the study of polite literature, which makes for meekness, makes needless also all further education; and we felt already as if the clouds that metaphysic had wrapped about the matter were dissolving in the light of a fresh and sweet intelligence. And, as we turned towards the dawn, we sighed over poor Hegel, who had read neither Goethe nor Homer, nor the Old and New Testaments, nor any of the literature which has gone to form "culture," but, knowing no facts, and reading no books, nor ever asking himself "such a tyro's question as what being really was," sat spinning out of his head those foolish logomachies which impose on no person of refinement.

Here is the identical weapon of Arnold, sharpened to a razor edge and turned against Arnold.

But the "stream" and the "tendency" having served their turn, like last week's placards, now fall into the background, and we learn at last that "the Eternal" is not eternal at all, unless we give that name to whatever a generation sees happen, and believes both has happened and will happen—just as the habit of washing ourselves might be termed "the Eternal not ourselves that makes for cleanliness," or "Early to bed and early to rise" the "Eternal not ourselves that makes for longevity," and so on—that "the Eternal," in short, is nothing in the world but a piece of literary clap-trap. The consequence is that all we are left with is the assertion that "righteousness" is "salvation" or welfare, and that there is a "law" and a "Power" which has something to do with this fact; and here again we must not be ashamed to say that we fail to understand what any one of these phrases means, and suspect ourselves once more to be on the scent of clap-trap.

A footnote continues the Arnold-baiting in a livelier style:

"Is there a God?" asks the reader. "Oh yes," replies Mr. Arnold, "and I can verify him in experience." "And what is he then?" cries the reader. "Be virtuous, and as a rule you will be happy," is the answer. "Well, and God?" "That is God," says Mr. Arnold; "there is no deception, and what more do you want?" I suppose we do want a good deal more. Most of us, certainly the public which Mr. Arnold addresses, want something they can worship; and they will not find that in an hypostasised copy-book heading, which is not much more adorable than "Honesty is the best policy," or "Handsome is that handsome does," or various other edifying maxims, which have not yet come to an apotheosis.

Such criticism is final. It is patently a great triumph of wit and a great delight to watch when a man's methods, almost his tricks of speech, are thus turned against himself. But if we look more closely into these words and into the whole chapter from which they are taken, we find Bradley to have been not only triumphant in polemic but right in reason. Arnold, with all his great virtues, was not always patient enough, or solicitous enough of any but immediate effect, to avoid inconsistency—as has been painstakingly shown by Mr. J. M. Robertson. In *Culture and Anarchy*, which is probably his greatest book, we hear something said about "the will of God"; but the "will of God" seems to become superseded in importance by "our best self, or right reason, to which we want to give authority"; and this best self looks very much like Matthew Arnold slightly disguised. In our own time one of the most remarkable of our critics, one who is fundamentally on most questions in the right, and very often right quite alone, Professor Irving Babbitt, has said again and again that the old curbs of class, of authoritative government, and of religion must be supplied in our time by something he calls the "inner check." The inner check looks very much like the "best self" of Matthew Arnold; and though supported by wider erudition and closer reasoning, is perhaps open to the same objections. There are words of Bradley's, and in the chapter from which we have already quoted, that might seem at first sight to support these two eminent doctrines:

How can the human-divine ideal ever be my will? The answer is, Your will it never can be as the will of your private self, so that your private self should become wholly good. To that self you must die, and by faith be made one with that ideal. You must resolve to give up your will, as the mere will of this or that man, and you must put your whole self, your entire will, into the will of the divine. That must be your one self, as it is your true self; that you must hold to both with thought and will, and all other you must renounce.

There is one direction in which these words—and, indeed, Bradley's philosophy as a whole—might be pushed, which would be dangerous; the direction of diminishing the value and dignity of the individual, of sacrificing him to a Church or a State. But, in any event, the words cannot be interpreted in the sense of Arnold. The distinction is not between a "private self" and a "public self" or a "higher self," it is between the individual as himself and no more, a mere numbered atom, and the individual in communion with God. The distinction is clearly drawn between man's "mere will" and "the will of the Divine." It may be noted also that Bradley is careful, in indicating the process, not to exaggerate either will or intellect at the expense of the other. And in all events it is a process which neither Arnold nor Professor Babbitt could accept. But *if* there is a "will of God," as Arnold, in a hasty moment, admits, then some doctrine of Grace must be admitted too; or else the "will of God" is just the same inoperative benevolence which we have all now and then received—and resented —from our fellow human beings. In the end it is a disappointment and a cheat.

Those who return to the reading of *Ethical Studies*, and those who now, after reading the other works of Bradley, read it for the first time, will be struck by the unity of Bradley's thought in the three books and in the collected Essays. But this unity is not the unity of mere fixity. In the *Ethical Studies*, for instance, he speaks of the awareness of the self, the knowledge of one's own existence as indubitable and identical. In *Appearance and Reality*, seventeen years later, he had seen much deeper into the matter; and had seen that no one "fact" of experience in isolation is real or is evidence of anything. The unity of Bradley's thought is not the unity attained by a man who never changes his mind. If he had so little occasion to change it, that is because he usually saw his problems from the beginning in all their complexity and connexions—saw them, in other words, with wisdom—and because he could never be deceived by his own metaphors— which, indeed, he used most sparingly—and was never tempted to make use of current nostrums.

If all of Bradley's writings are in some sense merely "essays," that is not solely a matter of modesty, or caution, and certainly not of in- ference, or even of ill-health. It is that he per- ceived the contiguity and continuity of the various provinces of thought. "Reflection on morality," he says, "leads us beyond it. It leads us, in short, to see the necessity of a religious point of view." Morality and religion are not the same thing, but they cannot beyond a cer- tain point be treated separately. A system of ethics, if thorough, is explicitly or implicitly a system of theology; and to attempt to erect a complete theory of ethics without a religion is none the less to adopt some particular attitude toward religion. In this book, as in his others, Bradley is thoroughly empirical, much more empirical than the philosophies that he opposed. He wished only to determine how much of morality could be founded securely without entering into the religious questions at all. As in *Appearance and Reality* he assumes that our common everyday knowledge is on the whole true so far as it goes, but that we do not know how far it does go; so in the *Ethical Studies* he starts always with the assumption that our common attitude toward duty, pleasure, or self-sacrifice is correct so far as it goes—but we do not know how far it does go. And in this he is all in the Greek tradition. It is fundamentally a philosophy of common sense.

Philosophy without wisdom is vain; and in the greater philosophers we are usually aware of that wisdom which for the sake of emphasis and in the most accurate and profound sense could be called even worldly wisdom. Common sense does not mean, of course, either the opinion of the majority or the opinion of the moment; it is not a thing to be got at without maturity and study and thought. The lack of it produces those unbalanced philosophies, such as Behaviourism, of which we hear a great deal. A purely "scientific" philosophy ends by denying what we know to be true; and, on the other hand, the great weakness of Pragmatism is that it ends by being of no *use* to anybody. Again, it is easy to underestimate Hegel, but it is easy to overestimate Bradley's debt to Hegel; in a philosophy like Bradley's the points at which he *stops* are always important points. In an unbalanced or uncultured philosophy words have a way of changing their meaning—as sometimes with Hegel; or else they are made, in a most ruthless and piratical manner, to walk the plank: the words which Professor J. B. Watson drops overboard, and which we know to have meaning and value, are almost innumerable. But Bradley, like Aristotle, is distinguished by his scrupulous respect for words, that their meaning should be neither vague nor exaggerated; and the tendency of his labours is to bring British philosophy closer to the great Greek tradition.

[88]

V.

BAUDELAIRE IN OUR TIME

Mr. Symons has made a good translation, in the Symons style.[1] If our point of view to-day was the point of view of thirty years ago, or even of twenty years ago, we should call it a good translation. To read Mr. Symons now, is to realize how great a man is Baudelaire, who can appear in such a different form to the 'nineties and to the nineteen-twenties. In the translation of Mr. Symons, Baudelaire becomes a poet of the 'nineties, a contemporary of Dowson and Wilde. Dowson and Wilde have passed, and Baudelaire remains; he belonged to a generation that preceded them, and yet he is much more our contemporary than are they. Yet even the 'nineties are nearer to us than the intervening generation—I date in *literary* generations; and the fact that they were interested in Baudelaire indicates some community of spirit. Since the generation—the *literary* generation—of Mr. Symons and the 'nineties, another generation has come and gone—the *literary* generation which includes Mr. Bernard Shaw, and Mr. Wells, and Mr. Lytton Strachey.

[1]Baudelaire, *Prose and Poetry*. Translated by Arthur Symons. Albert and Charles Boni.

This generation, in its ancestry, "skipped" the 'nineties: it is the progeny of Huxley, and Tyndall, and George Eliot, and Gladstone. And with this generation Baudelaire has nothing to do; but he had something to do with the 'nineties, and he has a great deal to do with us.

But the present volume should perhaps, even in fairness, be read as a document explicatory of the 'nineties, rather than as a current interpretation of Baudelaire. In an interesting preface—too short—Mr. Symons avows that the *Fleurs du Mal* "in regard to my earliest verses, was at once a fascination and an influence, and because from that time onward his fascination has been like a spell to me, and because that masterpiece has rarely, if ever, been equalled, has rarely, if ever, been surpassed." Mr. Symons is himself, we must remember, no mean poet; he is typical of the 'nineties; this influence of Baudelaire upon Mr. Symons was manifestly genuine and profound. Why is Baudelaire so different now? We can learn something about Baudelaire, and about the 'nineties, and about ourselves.

[92]

BAUDELAIRE IN OUR TIME

Mr. Symons's preface is very interesting: it is perhaps the most important part of the book. What is interesting is the attitude, so completely of his epoch, toward "vice." For Mr. Symons there is, at least *en principe*, a ritual, an hierarchy, a liturgy, of "vice" or "sin." Here is a whole paragraph so significant that I beg to give it entire:

In the poetry of Baudelaire, with which the poetry of Verlaine is so often compared [*i.e. compared by Mr. Symons and his friends—we no longer find much in common*] there is a deliberate science of sensual and sexual perversity which has something curious in its accentuation of vice with horror, in its passionate devotion to passions. Baudelaire brings every complication of taste, the exasperation of perfumes, the irritant of cruelty, the very odours and colours of corruption, to the creation and adornment of a sort of religion, in which an Eternal Mass is served before a veiled altar. There is no confession, no absolution, not a prayer is permitted which is not set down on the ritual. . . . "To cultivate one's hysteria" I have written "so calmly, and to affront the reader (*Hypocrite lecteur, mon semblable, mon frère*) as a judge rather than a penitent; to be a casuist in confession; to be so much a moralist, with so keen and so subtle a sense of the ecstasy of evil: that has always bewildered the world, even in his own country, where the artist is allowed to live as experimentally as he writes. Baudelaire lived and died solitary, secret, a confessor of sins who had never told the whole truth, *le mauvais moine* of his own sonnet, an ascetic of passion, a hermit of the Brothel."

This paragraph is of extraordinary interest for several reasons. Even in its cadences it conjures up Wilde and the remoter spectre of Pater. It conjures up also Lionel Johnson with his "life is a ritual." It cannot get away from religion and religious figures of speech. How different a tone from that of the generation of Mr. Shaw,[1] and Mr. Wells, and Mr. Strachey, and Mr. Ernest Hemingway! And how different from our own! Mr. Symons seems to us like a sensitive child, who has been taken into a church, and has been entranced with the effigies, and the candles, and the incense. *Such rugs and jugs and candle lights!*

---

[1] Of course Mr. Shaw and Mr. Wells are also much occupied with religion and *Ersatz-Religion*. But they are concerned with the spirit, not the letter. And the spirit killeth, but the letter giveth life.

And indeed the age of Mr. Symons was the "golden age" of one kind of child, as the age of Mr. Shaw was the age of another kind of child. If you take his paragraph to pieces, you will find much that is wrong; though if you swallow it whole, you will digest something that is right. *"Passionate devotion to passions"*: no man was ever less the dupe of passions than Baudelaire; he was engaged in an attempt to explain, to justify, to make something of them, an enterprise which puts him almost on a level with the author of the "Vita Nuova." *"The irritant of cruelty"*—did Baudelaire "bring" it, or did he not merely examine it (there are some important paragraphs in *Mon Coeur Mis à Nu*). Whoever heard of a Mass before a veiled altar? And hysteria! was any one ever less hysterical, more lucid, than Baudelaire?[1] There is a difference between hysteria and looking into the Shadow. And when Mr. Symons says, a few pages later, that Baudelaire's "impeccable" work is "the

----

[1] It is true that Baudelaire says *"J'ai cultivé mon hystérie."* But it is one thing for him to say it of himself, another for Mr. Symons to say it about him.

direct result of his heredity and of his nerves"
I can only protest violently. If any work is to
be described as the "direct" result of heredity
and nerves—and "direct" here can only suggest
that heredity and nerves sufficiently account
for the work—then I cannot agree that such
work is impeccable. We cannot be *primarily*
interested in any writer's nerves (and remember
please that "nerves" used in this way is a very
vague and unscientific term) or in any one's
heredity except for the purpose of knowing to
what extent that writer's individuality distorts
or detracts from the objective truth which he
perceives. If a writer sees truly—as far as he
sees at all—then his heredity and nerves do
not matter.[1] What is right in Mr. Symons's
account is the impression it gives that Baudelaire was primarily occupied with religious
values. What is wrong is the childish attitude
of the 'nineties toward religion, the belief—
which is no more than the game of children
dressing up and playing at being grown-ups

[1]There is a better, and very interesting, account of Baudelaire's heredity in Léon Daudet's book, *L'Hérédo*.

—that there is a religion of Evil, or Vice, or Sin. Swinburne knew nothing about Evil, or Vice, or Sin—if he had known anything he would not have had so much fun out of it. For Swinburne's disciples, the men of the 'nineties, Evil was very good fun. Experience, as a sequence of outward events, is nothing in itself; it is possible to pass through the most terrible experiences protected by histrionic vanity; Wilde, through the whole of the experiences of his life, remained a little Eyas, a child-actor. On the other hand, even to act an important thing is to acknowledge it; and the childishness of the 'nineties is nearer to reality than the childishness of the nineteen-hundreds. But to Baudelaire, alone, these things were real.

Mr. Symons appears a more childish child than Huysmans, merely because a childish Englishman—bred a Protestant—always appears more childish than a childish Frenchman —bred a Roman. Huysmans's fee-fi-fo-fum *décor* of mediævalism has nothing on Mr. Symons's "veiled altar." Huysmans, by the way,

might have been much more in sympathy with
the real spirit of the thirteenth century if he
had thought less about it, and bothered less
about architectural lore and quotations from
philosophers whom he may have read but certainly did not understand: he is much more
"mediæval" (and much more human) when he
describes the visit of Madame Chantelouve
to Durtal than when he talks about his
Cathedral.

I have already suggested that Mr. Symons,
as a translator, turns Baudelaire into a contemporary of Symons. To say this is at once a very
high compliment—for the work of translation
is to make something foreign, or something remote in time, live with our own life, and no
translator can endow his victim with more
abundant life than he possesses himself—and
a warning. It is not a warning against Mr.
Symons as translator. Mr. Symons is as true a
translator as Mr. Symons can be. That is to
say that his translation is, from his own point
of view, almost perfect; we have no suggestions
to make to Mr. Symons himself. Only, it is

what Baudelaire means to Mr. Symons's generation; it is not what Baudelaire means to us. For one thing, we now are much better qualified to appreciate the very traditional character of Baudelaire's verse; we are nearer to Racine than is Mr. Symons; and if we translated Baudelaire ourselves we should bring out just those resemblances to Racine, which disappear completely in Mr. Symons's translation. It is a pity that Mr. Symons has not translated some of the poems in which this affinity with Racine is most apparent. The poet who wrote

Andromaque, des bras d'un grand époux tombée,
Vil bétail, sous la main du superbe Pyrrhus . . .

De l'ancien Frascati vestale enamourée . . .

Nos Pylades là-bas tendent leurs bras vers nous.
"Pour rafraîchir ton coeur nage vers ton Electre !" . . .

is not remote from the poet who wrote of *"La fille de Minos et Pasiphaë . . ."* We can, however, call attention to passages where it seems to us that Mr. Symons has enveloped Baudelaire in the Swinburnian violet-coloured London fog of the 'nineties. His paraphrase of "L'Invitation au Voyage" is significant.

> My child and my star,
> Let us wander afar . . .

Baudelaire wrote

> *Mon enfant, ma soeur,*
> *Songe à la douceur*
> *D'aller là-bas vivre ensemble.*

The word *soeur* here is not, in my opinion, chosen merely because it rhymes with *douceur;* it is a moment in that sublimation of passion toward which Baudelaire was always striving; it needs a commentary out of his Correspondence, for instance the astonishing letter to Marie X . . . cited by Charles Du Bos.[1] (On this whole subject Du Bos, whose essay on Baudelaire is the finest study of Baudelaire that has been made, has some admirable words: *ce désir contemplatif qui n'a besoin que de la présence, et qui ne possède vraiment que parce qu'il ne possède pas.*)

---

[1]Charles Du Bos, *Approximations*, p. 219.

And further on, in the same poem, when we come to the magnificent lines

> *Là, tout n'est qu'ordre et beauté,*
> *Luxe, calme et volupté*

we are surprised to receive from Mr. Symons

> There all is beauty, ardency,
> Passion, rest and luxury.

The only one of these words that is right is "beauty." Baudelaire did not, we may be sure, take these substantives at random, nor did he arrange them at random. It is not for nothing that he put *ordre* first; and if Mr. Symons had understood *notre* Baudelaire he would not have substituted—"ardency"! But order is positive, chaos is defect, and we imagine that Mr. Symons was not trying to *avoid* Order—he simply did not recognize it. We can see that Mr. Symons, trained in the verbal school of Swinburne, is simply anxious to get a nice sounding phrase; and we infer that all that he found in Baudelaire was a nice sounding phrase.

But Baudelaire was not a disciple of Swinburne: for Baudelaire every word counts.

Here is another passage where Mr. Symons seems to me merely to have made a smudgy botch. It is striking because it is Baudelaire in his most sardonic, bathetic vein—something which might be called strictly "modern," and which should therefore (considering that Mr. Symons belongs to a younger generation than Baudelaire) have appealed to Mr. Symons. These are well-known lines from the "Voyage à Cythère."

> *Quelle est cette île triste et noire? C'est Cythère,*
> *Nous dit-on, un pays fameux dans les chansons,*
> *Eldorado banal de tous les vieux garçons.*
> *Regardez, après tout, c'est une pauvre terre.*

Mr. Symons astounds us with the following:

What is this sad dark Isle? It is Cythera whose birth
Was famed in songs, made famous as the fashions
Of the most ancient and adulterous passions:
It is a beautiful and a barren earth.

Here Mr. Symons's "stretchèd metre," always reminiscent of Cynara, fits Baudelaire's delib-

erately broken alexandrines better than it does
in many places (in many of the poems, one feels
that Pope would have been better fitted than
Mr. Symons). But such a mistranslation cannot be merely a confession of impotence to
translate the words of Baudelaire into English;
it expresses an impotence to *feel* the moods of
Baudelaire—they can be expressed in English
just as well as in French—an impotence to use
words definitely, to use words at all unless they
are the few poor counters of habitual and lazy
sentiment. *Fashions and Passions*—how well we
know them!

The important fact about Baudelaire is that
he was essentially a Christian, born out of his
due time, and a classicist, born out of his due
time. In his verse technique, he is nearer to
Racine than to Mr. Symons; in his sensibility,
he is near to Dante and not without sympathy
with Tertullian. But Baudelaire was not an
æsthetic or a political Christian; his tendency
to "ritual," which Mr. Symons, with his highly
acute but blind sensibility, has observed, springs
from no attachment to the outward forms of

Christianity, but from the instincts of a soul that was *naturaliter* Christian. And being the kind of Christian that he was, born when he was, he had to discover Christianity for himself. In this pursuit he was alone in the solitude which is only known to saints. To him the notion of Original Sin came spontaneously; and the need for prayer.

Tout chez Baudelaire est fonction de son génie; or il n'y a rien dont ce génie puisse moins se passer que de Dieu, —d'un Dieu qui plutôt qu'objet de foi est réceptacle de prières,—j'irai jusqu'à dire d'un Dieu qu'on puisse prier sans croire en lui. . . . Cet incoercible besoin de prière au sein même de l'incrédulité,—signe majeur d'une âme marquée de christianisme, qui jamais ne lui échappera tout à fait. La notion de péché, et plus profondement encore le besoin de prière, telles sont les deux réalités souterraines qui paraissent appartenir à des gisements enfouis bien plus avant que ne l'est la foi elle-même. On se rappelle le mot de Flaubert: "Je suis mystique au fond et je ne crois à rien"; Baudelaire et lui se sont toujours fraternellement compris.

So far Charles Du Bos. Other essays, not so satisfactory as that of M. Du Bos, but recent and explanatory of Baudelaire, as he is now understood, are "Notre Baudelaire" by Stanislas Fumet, and "La Vie Douloureuse de Baudelaire" by François Porché.

And Baudelaire came to attain the greatest, the most difficult, of the Christian virtues, the virtue of humility. Only by devoted study of the man and his work and his life can we appreciate the significance of that great passage in *Mon Coeur Mis à Nu:*

Faire tous les matins ma prière à Dieu, réservoir de toute force et de toute justice, à mon père, à Mariette et à Poë, comme intercesseurs; les prier de me communiquer la force nécessaire pour accomplir tous mes devoirs, et d'octroyer à ma mère une vie assez longue pour jouir de ma transformation; travailler toute la journée, ou du moins tant que mes forces me le permettront; me fier à Dieu, c'est-à-dire à la Justice même, pour la réussite de mes projets; faire, tous les soirs, une nouvelle prière, pour demander à Dieu la vie et la force pour ma mère et pour moi, faire, de tout ce que je gagnerai, quatre parts,—une pour la vie courante, une pour mes créanciers, une pour mes amis et une pour ma mère;—obéir aux principes de la plus stricte sobriété, dont le premier est la suppression de tous les excitants, quels qu'ils soient.

VI.

THOMAS MIDDLETON

THOMAS MIDDLETON, THE DRAMATIC WRITER, was not very highly thought of in his own time; the date of his death is not known; we know only that he was buried on July 4, 1627. He was one of the more voluminous, and one of the best, dramatic writers of his time. But it is easy to understand why he is not better known or more popular. It is difficult to imagine his "personality." Several new personalities have recently been fitted to the name of Shakespeare; Jonson is a real figure—our imagination plays about him discoursing at the Mermaid, or laying down the law to Drummond of Hawthornden; Chapman has become a breezy British character as firm as Nelson or Wellington; Webster and Donne are real people for the more intellectual; even Tourneur (Churton Collins having said the last word about him) is a "personality." But Middleton, who collaborated shamelessly, who is hardly separated from Rowley, Middleton, who wrote plays so diverse as *Women Beware Women* and *A Game at Chesse* and *The Roaring Girl*, Middleton remains merely a collective name for a number of plays—some

[109]

of which, like *The Spanish Gypsy*, are patently by other people.[1]

If we write about Middleton's plays we must write about Middleton's plays, and not about Middleton's personality. Many of these plays are still in doubt. Of all the Elizabethan dramatists Middleton seems the most impersonal, the most indifferent to personal fame or perpetuity, the readiest, except Rowley, to accept collaboration. Also he is the most various. His greatest tragedies and his greatest comedies are as if written by two different men. Yet there seems no doubt that Middleton was both a great comic writer and a great tragic writer. There are a sufficient number of plays, both tragedies and comedies, in which his hand is so far unquestioned, to establish his greatness. His greatness is not that of a peculiar personality, but of a great artist or artisan of the Elizabethan epoch. We have among others *The Changeling*, *Women Beware Women*, and *A Game at Chesse;* and we have *The Roaring Girl* and *A Trick to Catch the*

---

[1]Mr. Dugdale Sykes has written authoritatively on this subject.

Old One. And that is enough. Between the tragedies and the comedies of Shakespeare, and certainly between the tragedies and the comedies of Jonson, we can establish a relation; we can see, for Shakespeare or Jonson, that each had in the end a personal point of view which can be called neither comic nor tragic. But with Middleton we can establish no such relation. He remains merely a name, a voice, the author of certain plays, which are all of them great plays. He has no point of view, is neither sentimental nor cynical; he is neither resigned, nor disillusioned, nor romantic; he has no message. He is merely the name which associates six or seven great plays.

For there is no doubt about *The Changeling*. Like all of the plays attributed to Middleton, it is long-winded and tiresome; the characters talk too much, and then suddenly stop talking and act; they are real and impelled irresistibly by the fundamental motions of humanity to good or evil. This mixture of tedious discourse and sudden reality is everywhere in the work of Middleton, in his comedy also. In *The Roaring*

[111]

Girl we read with toil through a mass of cheap conventional intrigue, and suddenly realize that we are, and have been for some time without knowing it, observing a real and unique human being. In reading *The Changeling* we may think, till almost the end of the play, that we have been concerned merely with a fantastic Elizabethan morality, and then discover that we are looking on at an impassionate exposure of fundamental passions of any time and any place. The usual opinion remains the just judgment: *The Changeling* is Middleton's greatest play. The morality of the convention seems to us absurd. To many intelligent readers this play has only an historical interest, and only serves to illustrate the moral taboos of the Elizabethans. The heroine is a young woman who, in order to dispose of a fiancé to whom she is indifferent, so that she may marry the man she loves, accepts the offer of an adventurer to murder the affianced, at the price of becoming the murderer's mistress. Such a plot is, to a modern mind, absurd; and the consequent tragedy seems a fuss about nothing. But *The*

Changeling is not merely contingent for its effect upon our acceptance of Elizabethan good form or convention; it is, in fact, no more dependent upon the convention of its epoch than a play like *A Doll's House*. Underneath the convention there is the stratum of permanent truth to human nature. The tragedy of *The Changeling* is an eternal tragedy, as permanent as *Œdipus* or *Anthony and Cleopatra;* it is the tragedy of the not naturally bad but irresponsible and undeveloped nature, caught in the consequences of its own action. In every age and in every civilization there are instances of the same thing: the unmoral nature, suddenly trapped in the inexorable toils of morality— of morality not made by man but by Nature— and forced to take the consequences of an act which it had planned light-heartedly. Beatrice is not a moral creature; she becomes moral only by becoming damned. Our conventions are not the same as those which Middleton assumed for his play. But the possibility of that frightful discovery of morality remains permanent.

The words in which Middleton expresses

his tragedy are as great as the tragedy. The process through which Beatrice, having decided that De Flores is the instrument for her purpose, passes from aversion to habituation, remains a permanent commentary on human nature. The directness and precision of De Flores are masterly, as is also the virtuousness of Beatrice on first realizing his motives—

> Why, 'tis impossible thou canst be so wicked,
> Or shelter such a cunning cruelty,
> To make his death the murderer of my honour!
> Thy language is so bold and vicious,
> I cannot see which way I can forgive it
> With any modesty

—a passage which ends with the really great lines of De Flores, lines of which Shakespeare or Sophocles might have been proud:

Can you weep Fate from its determined purpose?
So soon may you weep me.

But what constitutes the essence of the tragedy is something which has not been sufficiently remarked; it is the *habituation* of Beatrice to

[114]

her sin; it becomes no longer sin but merely custom. Such is the essence of the tragedy of *Macbeth*—the habituation to crime, the deadening of all moral sense. And in the end Beatrice, having been so long the enforced conspirator of De Flores, becomes (and this is permanently true to human nature) more *his* partner, *his* mate, than the mate and partner of the man for the love of whom she consented to the crime. Her lover disappears not only from the scene but from her own imagination. When she says of De Flores,

> A wondrous necessary man, my lord,

her praise is more than half sincere; and at the end she belongs far more to De Flores— toward whom, at the beginning, she felt strong physical repulsion—than to her lover Alsemero. It is De Flores, in the end, to whom she belongs as Francesca to Paolo:

> Beneath the stars, upon yon meteor
> Ever hung my fate, 'mongst things corruptible;
> I ne'er could pluck it from him; my loathing
> Was prophet to the rest, but ne'er believed.

And De Flores's cry is perfectly sincere and in character:

> I loved this woman in spite of her heart;
> Her love I earned out of Piracquo's murder . . .
> Yes, and her honour's prize
> Was my reward; I thank life for nothing
> But that pleasure; it was so sweet to me,
> That I have drunk up all, left none behind
> For any man to pledge me.

The tragedy of Beatrice is not that she has lost Alsemero, for whose possession she played; it is that she has won De Flores. Such tragedies are not limited to Elizabethan times: they happen every day and perpetually. The greatest tragedies are occupied with great and permanent moral conflicts: the great tragedies of Æschylus, of Sophocles, of Corneille, of Racine, of Shakespeare have the same burden. In poetry, in dramatic technique, *The Changeling* is inferior to the best plays of Webster. But in the moral essence of tragedy it is safe to say that in this play Middleton is surpassed by one Elizabethan alone, and that is Shakespeare. In some respects in which Elizabethan tragedy can be compared to French or to Greek tragedy *The Changeling* stands above every tragic play of its time, except those of Shakespeare.

The genius which blazed in *The Changeling* was fitful but not accidental. The best tragedy after *The Changeling* is *Women Beware Women*. The thesis of the play, as the title indicates, is more arbitrary and less fundamental. The play itself, although less disfigured by ribaldry or clowning, is more tedious. Middleton sinks himself in conventional moralizing of the epoch, so that, if we are impatient, we decide that he gives merely a document of Elizabethan humbug—and then suddenly a personage will blaze out in genuine fire of vituperation. The wickedness of the personages in *Women Beware Women* is conventional wickedness of the stage of the time; yet slowly the exasperation of Bianca, the wife who married beneath her, beneath the ambitions to which she was entitled, emerges from the negative; slowly the real human passions emerge from the mesh of interest in which they begin. And here again Middleton, in writing what appears on the surface a conventional picture-palace Italian melodrama of the time, has caught permanent human feelings. And in this play Middleton shows his interest—more than any of his contemporaries —in innuendo and double meanings; and makes use of that game of chess, which he was to use more openly and directly for satire in that perfect piece of literary political art, *A Game at Chesse*. The irony could not be improved upon:

Did I not say my duke would fetch you o'er, Wiaow?
I think you spoke in earnest when you said it, madam.
And my black king makes all the haste he can too.
Well, madam, we may meet with him in time yet.
I've given thee blind mate twice.

There is hardly anything truer or more impressive in Elizabethan drama than Bianca's gradual self-will and self-importance in consequence of her courtship by the Duke:

Troth, you speak wondrous well for your old house here;
'Twill shortly fall down at your feet to thank you,
Or stoop, when you go to bed, like a good child,
To ask you blessing.

[118]

In spite of all the long-winded speeches, in spite of all the conventional Italianate horrors, Bianca remains, like Beatrice in *The Changeling*, a real woman; as real, indeed, as any woman of Elizabethan tragedy. Bianca is a type of the woman who is purely moved by vanity.

But if Middleton, this obscure and uninteresting person, understood the female better than any of the Elizabethans—better than the creator of the Duchess of Malfy, better than Marlowe, better than Tourneur, or Shirley, or Fletcher, better than any of them except Shakespeare alone—he was also able, in his comedy, to present a finer woman than any of them. *The Roaring Girl* has no apparent relation to Middleton's tragedies, yet it is agreed to be primarily the work of Middleton. It is typical of the comedies of Middleton, and it is the best. In his tragedies Middleton employs all the Italianate horrors of his time, and obviously for the purpose of pleasing the taste of his time; yet underneath we feel always a quiet and undisturbed vision of things as they are and not "another thing." So in his comedies. The comedies are long-winded; the fathers are heavy fathers, and rant as heavy fathers should; the sons are wild and wanton sons, and perform all the pranks to be expected of them; the machinery is the usual Elizabethan machinery; Middleton is solicitous to please his audience with what they expect; but there is underneath the same steady impersonal passionless observation of human nature. *The Roaring Girl* is as artificial as any comedy of the time; its plot creaks loudly; yet the Girl herself is always real. She may rant, she may behave preposterously, but she remains a type of the sort of woman who has renounced all happiness for herself and who lives only for a principle. Nowhere more than in *The Roaring Girl* can the hand of Middleton be distinguished more clearly from the hand of Dekker. Dekker is all sentiment; and, indeed, in the so admired passages of *A Fair Quarrel*, exploited by Lamb, the mood if not the hand of Dekker seems to the unexpert critic to be more present than Middleton's. *A Fair Quarrel* seems as much, if not more, Dekker's than Middleton's. Similarly with *The Spanish Gypsy*, which can with difficulty be attributed to Middleton. But the feeling about Moll Cut-Purse of *The Roaring Girl* is Middleton's rather than anybody's. In Middleton's tragedy there is a strain of realism underneath, which is one with the poetry; and in his comedy we find the same thing.

In her recent book on *The Social Mode of Restoration Comedy*, Miss Kathleen Lynch calls attention to the gradual transition from Elizabethan-Jacobean to Restoration comedy. She observes, what is certainly true, that Middleton is the greatest "realist" in Jacobean comedy. Miss Lynch's extremely suggestive thesis is that the transition from Elizabethan-Jacobean to later Caroline comedy is primarily economic: that the interest changes from the citizen aping gentry to the citizen become gentry and accepting that code of manners. In the comedy of Middleton certainly there is as yet no code of manners; but the merchant of Cheapside is *aiming* at becoming a member of the county gentry. Miss Lynch remarks: "Middleton's keen concentration on the spectacle of the interplay of different social classes marks an important development in realistic comedy." She calls attention to this aspect of Middleton's comedy, that it marks, better than the romantic comedy of Shakespeare, or the comedy of Jonson, occupied with what Jonson thought to be permanent and not transient aspects of human nature, the transition between the aristocratic world which preceded the Tudors and the plutocratic modern world which the Tudors initiated and encouraged. By the time of the return of Charles II, as Miss Lynch points out, society had been reorganized and formed, and social conventions had been created. In the Tudor times birth still counted (though nearly all the great families were extinct); by the time of Charles II only breeding counted. The comedy of Middleton, and the comedy of Brome, and the comedy of Shirley, is intermediate, as Miss Lynch remarks. Middleton, she observes, marks the transitional stage in which the London tradesman was anxious to cease to be a tradesman and to become a country gentleman. The words of his City Magnate in

Michaelmas Terme have not yet lost their point:

A fine journey in the Whitsun holydays, i'faith, to ride with a number of citizens and their wives, some upon pillions, some upon side-saddles, I and little Thomasine i' the middle, our son and heir, Sim Quomodo, in a peach-colour taffeta jacket, some horse length, or a long yard before us—there will be a fine show on's I can tell you.

But Middleton's comedy is not, like the comedy of Congreve, the comedy of a set social behaviour; it is still, like the later comedy of Dickens, the comedy of individuals, in spite of the continual motions of city merchants toward county gentility. In the comedy of the Restoration a figure such as that of Moll Cut-Purse would have been impossible. As a social document the comedy of Middleton illustrates the transition from government by a landed aristocracy to government by a city aristocracy gradually engrossing the land. As such it is of the greatest interest. But as literature, as a dispassionate picture of human nature, Middleton's comedy deserves to be remembered chiefly by its real—perpetually real—and human

[123]

figure of Moll the Roaring Girl. That Middleton's comedy was "photographic," that it introduces us to the low life of the time far better than anything in the comedy of Shakespeare or the comedy of Jonson, better than anything except the pamphlets of Dekker and Greene and Nashe, there is little doubt. But it produced one great play—*The Roaring Girl*—a great play in spite of the tedious long speeches of some of the principal characters, in spite of the clumsy machinery of the plot: for the reason that Middleton was a great observer of human nature, without fear, without sentiment, without prejudice, without personality.

And Middleton in the end—after criticism has subtracted all that Rowley, all that Dekker, all that others contributed—is a great example of great English drama. He has no message; he is merely a great recorder. Incidentally, in flashes and when the dramatic need comes, he is a great poet, a great master of versification:

I that am of your blood was taken from you
For your better health; look no more upon 't,
But cast it to the ground regardlessly,

THOMAS MIDDLETON

Let the common sewer take it from distinction:
Beneath the stars, upon yon meteor
Ever hung my fate, 'mongst things corruptible;
I ne'er could pluck it from him; my loathing
Was prophet to the rest, but ne'er believed.

The man who wrote these lines remains inscrutable, solitary, unadmired; purely an Elizabethan and not himself; welcoming collaboration, indifferent to fame; dying no one knows when and no one knows how; attracting, in three hundred years, no personal admiration. Yet he wrote one tragedy which more than any play except those of Shakespeare has a profound and permanent moral value and horror; and one comedy which more than any Elizabethan comedy realizes a free and noble womanhood.

VII.

A NOTE ON RICHARD CRASHAW

No HIGHER COMPLIMENT CAN BE PAID TO THIS book[1] than to say that in editing and in production it is worthy of the fine series of seventeenth-century poets of which it is a member. Memorable in this series are Saintsbury's "Caroline Poets" (without which Benlowes, Cleveland, and King would be almost inaccessible), Grierson's "Donne," Margoliouth's "Marvell," and Professor Martin's own "Vaughan." This edition of Crashaw was much needed. Heretofore the only scholarly edition was that of Waller, in 1904. It was a good edition for its time; but the text was neither well established nor complete; and for an ordinary reader it had the disadvantage that one sometimes had to hunt to find the poem one wanted. Mr. Martin has collated the texts and gives the variants, without disfiguring the pages of a very handsome and practical book. His notes deserve particular attention, for Crashaw is a poet who needs notes—not for reading for pleasure—but if we wish to study him in relation to his time. Poets of that age made use of each other pretty freely;

---

[1] *The Poems English Latin and Greek of Richard Crashaw*. Edited by L. C. Martin. Oxford University Press.

Crashaw for one was well read (thanks partly to his father's library) in the Italian and Latin poetry of his time, which was Legion. Mr. Martin's notes give many interesting parallels. If there is anything more to be discovered about Crashaw, it will be in the way of further derivations.

Having given due praise to the edition, I must confess to some disappointment with the introduction. It gives a very dense summary of the facts, and includes an extremely interesting letter written by Crashaw. But Mr. Martin seems over-anxious not to use too much space: on the other hand the one critical opinion on which he ventures does not seem to me happy. Perhaps I expected, in default of any critical biography of Crashaw, something that would take its place; something as good as Grierson's capital study of Donne in his edition of that poet above mentioned. We are still left with no first-rate criticism of Crashaw in English. The best study of Crashaw that I know, and a very fine and suggestive essay, is that by Mario Praz in his *Secentismo e Marinismo in Inghilterra*.

A NOTE ON RICHARD CRASHAW

"When we survey," says Professor Martin, "the remarkable development of Crashaw's genius close up to the end of his life, in circumstances that must often have been trying and distracting in the extreme, his 'unfulfilled renown' becomes indeed comparable with that of those other two English poets whose work his own in some ways strangely foreshadows, and who, like him, found in Italy a retreat and a final resting place." (I wish Mr. Martin had saved a line or two by saying Keats and Shelley straight out, instead of searching for a fine phrase.) Now this remark might lead to several false inferences. Crashaw lived to be about thirty-seven; so he had some good years more than Keats or Shelley in which to develop. A man can go far between twenty-seven and thirty-seven. Mr. Martin is therefore unfair to Keats and Shelley. But moreover Crashaw's verse is, as one would expect, far more mature than that of either of these poets; and I do not find in the poem on which he bases this suggestion, the "Letter to the Countess of Denbigh," the evidence of *promise* that Mr. Martin finds in it. It is indeed a fine poem, but it is the work of a mature master, and promises nothing but more of the same kind. Crashaw is, I believe, a much greater poet than he is usually supposed to be; Keats and Shelley are, in their actual accomplishment, not nearly such great poets as they are supposed to be. But nothing that Crashaw wrote has the *promise* that is patent in *Hyperion* or *The Triumph of Life*. We must try of course always to distinguish promise from performance; both must be taken into account in judging a poet, and they must be kept separate. We can only say that Keats and Shelley would *probably* have become greater poets, poets on a much greater scale, than Crashaw; judging them on their accomplishment only, Crashaw was a finished master, and Keats and Shelley were apprentices with immense possibilities before them.

So much for one question. Next, in what way can Crashaw be said to "foreshadow" Keats and Shelley? As for Keats, I simply do not know what Mr. Martin means, I see so little resemblance. With Shelley, there are obvious

and striking resemblances, though I think very
superficial ones. To suggest, as Mr. Martin's
words seem to me to suggest, that Crashaw
was in any way a forerunner or "prophet" of
Shelley, is quite off the rails. The obvious
parallel is between "The Weeper" and "The
Skylark," rather than between their uses of
the octosyllabic couplet, which are wholly
different.

> The dew no more will weepe,
>   The Primroses pale cheeke to decke,
>   The deaw no more will sleepe,
>   Nuzzel'd in the Lillies neck.
> Much rather would it tremble heere,
> And leave them both to bee thy Teare.

> Not the soft Gold which
>   Steales from the Amber-weeping Tree,
>   Makes sorrow halfe so Rich,
>   As the drops distil'd from thee.
> Sorrowes best Iewels lye in these
> Caskets, of which Heaven keeps the Keyes.

> .   .   .   .   .

> Not in the Evenings Eyes
>   When they red with weeping are,
>   For the Sun that dyes,
>   Sits sorrow with a face so faire.

FOR LANCELOT ANDREWES

Nowhere but heere did ever meet
Sweetnesse so sad, sadnes so sweet.

I doubt whether the *sound* of two poems can
be very similar, when the *sense* is entirely different. At any rate, I have found that the more I
studied the meaning of Crashaw's verse, and
his peculiar use of image and conceit, the less
resemblance the music of it seemed to have to
Shelley's. Take one of Crashaw's more extreme
and grotesque figures, from "The Tear":

> Faire Drop, why quak'st thou so?
> 'Cause thou streight must lay thy Head
> In the Dust? o no;
> The Dust shall never bee thy Bed:
> A pillow for thee will I bring,
> Stuft with Downe of Angels wing.

This imagery is almost the quintessence of an
immense mass of devotional verse of the seventeenth century. But it has nothing to do with
Shelley. Crashaw's images, even when entirely
preposterous—for there is no warrant for bring-
ing a pillow (and what a pillow!) for the *head*
of a *tear*—give a kind of intellectual pleasure—

it is a deliberate conscious perversity of language, a perversity like that of the amazing and amazingly impressive interior of St. Peter's. There is brain work in it. But in "The Skylark" there is no brain work. For the first time perhaps in verse of such eminence, sound exists without sense. Crashaw would never have written so shabby a line as "That from heaven or near it" merely to provide an imperfect rhyme for *spirit*.

> Keen as are the arrows
>   Of that silver sphere
> Whose intense lamp narrows
>   In the white dawn clear,
> Until we hardly see, we feel that it is there.

I should be grateful for any explanation of this stanza; until now I am still ignorant to what Sphere Shelley refers, or why it should have silver arrows, or what the devil he means by an intense lamp narrowing in the white dawn; though I can understand that we could hardly see the lamp of a *silver* sphere narrowing in *white* dawn (why dawn? as he has just referred

to the pale purple even). There may be some
clue for persons more learned than I; but Shelley should have provided notes. Crashaw does
not need *such* notes.

And when Shelley has some definite statement to make, he simply says it; keeps his
images on one side and his meanings on the
other:

> We look before and after,
>   And pine for what is not:
> Our sincerest laughter
>   With some pain is fraught;
> Our sweetest songs are those that tell of saddest
>   thought.

This is a sweeping assertion, and is rather com-
monplace in expression; but it is intelligible.
And it is not in the least like Crashaw.

I call Crashaw a "devotional" poet, because
the word "religious" is so abused. Shelley even
has been called religious, but he could not be
called devout; he is religious in the same sense
as when we say that Dean Inge or the Bishop
of Birmingham is religious. Devotional poetry
is religious poetry which falls within an ex-

act faith and has precise objects for contemplation. Crashaw is sometimes called erotic in his devotion. "Erotic" is an abused word, but in any case ought not to be an offensive word. In one aspect it may be applied to Crashaw. Dante, for instance, always seems perfectly aware of every shade of both human and divine love; Beatrice is his means of transition between the two; and there is never any danger of his confounding the two loves. But just as Crashaw is deficient in humanity, and yet is neither quite in the world nor out of it, and so is neither a Dante nor an Adam of St. Victor, so we feel at times that his passion for heavenly objects is imperfect because it is partly a substitute for human passion. It is not impure, but it is incomplete.

Yet Crashaw is quite alone in his peculiar kind of greatness. He is alone among the metaphysical poets of England, who were mostly intensely English: Crashaw is primarily a European. He was saturated still more in Italian and Latin poetry than in English. Indeed Mr. Mario Praz, who has probably read more than anybody of the Latin poetry and the continental poetry of the seventeenth century, puts Crashaw above Marino, Góngora, and everybody else, merely as the *representative* of the baroque spirit in literature.

VIII.

THE HUMANISM OF
IRVING BABBITT

IT IS PROVERBIALLY EASIER TO DESTROY THAN to construct; and as a corollary of this proverb, it is easier for readers to apprehend the destructive than the constructive side of an author's thought. More than this: when a writer is skilful at destructive criticism, the public is satisfied with that. If he has no constructive philosophy, it is not demanded; and if he has, it is overlooked. This is especially true when we are concerned with critics of society, from Arnold to the present day. All such critics are criticized from one common standard, and that the lowest: the standard of brilliant attack upon aspects of contemporary society which we know and dislike. It is the easiest standard to take. For the criticism deals with concrete things in our world which we know, and the writer may be merely echoing, in neater phrasing, our own thoughts; whereas the construction deals with things hard and unfamiliar. Hence the popularity of Mr. Mencken.

But there are more serious critics than Mr. Mencken, and of these we must ask in the end what they have to offer in place of what they denounce. M. Julien Benda, for instance, makes it a part of his deliberate programme to offer nothing; he has a romantic view of critical detachment which limits his interest. Mr. Wyndham Lewis is obviously striving courageously toward a positive theory, but in his published work has not yet reached that point. But in Professor Babbitt's latest book, *Democracy and Leadership*, the criticism is related to a positive theory and dependent upon it. This theory is not altogether expounded, but is partly assumed. What I wish to do in the present essay is to ask a few questions of Mr. Babbitt's constructive theory.

The centre of Mr. Babbitt's philosophy is the doctrine of humanism. In his earlier books we were able to accept this idea without analysis; but in *Democracy and Leadership*—which I take to be at this point the summary of his theory—we are tempted to question it. The problem of humanism is undoubtedly related to the problem of religion. Mr. Babbitt makes it very clear, here and there throughout the book, that he is unable to take the religious view—that is to say that he cannot accept any dogma or

[142]

revelation; and that humanism is the *alternative* to religion. And this brings up the question: is this alternative any more than a *substitute*, and if a substitute, does it not bear the same relation to religion that "humanitarianism" bears to humanism? Is it, in the end, a view of life that will work by itself, or is it a derivative of religion which will work only for a short time in history, and only for a few highly cultivated persons like Mr. Babbitt—whose ancestral traditions, furthermore, are Christian, and who is, like many people, at the distance of a generation or so from definite Christian belief? Is it, in other words, durable beyond one or two generations?

Mr. Babbitt says, of the "representatives of the humanitarian movement," that

they wish to live on the naturalistic level, and at the same time to enjoy the benefits that the past had hoped to achieve as a result of some humanistic or religious discipline.

The definition is admirable, but provokes us to ask whether, by altering a few words, we cannot arrive at the following statement about humanists:

they wish to live on the humanistic level, and at the same time to enjoy the benefits that the past had hoped to achieve as a result of some religious discipline.

If this transposition is justified, it means that the difference is only of one step: the humanitarian has suppressed the properly human, and is left with the animal; the humanist has suppressed the divine, and is left with a human element which may quickly descend again to the animal from which he has sought to raise it.

Mr. Babbitt is a stout upholder of tradition and continuity, and he knows, with all his immense and encyclopedic information, that the Christian religion is an essential part of the history of our race. Humanism and religion are thus, as historical facts, by no means parallel; humanism has been sporadic, but Christianity continuous. It is quite irrelevant to conjecture the possible development of the European races without Christianity—to imagine, that is, a tradition of humanism equivalent to the actual tradition of Christianity. For all we can say is that we should have been very different creatures, whether better or worse. Our problem being to form the future, we can only form it on the materials of the past; we must *use* our heredity, instead of denying it. The religious habits of the race are still very strong, in all places, at all times, and for all people. There is no humanistic habit: humanism is, I think, merely the state of mind of a few persons in a few places at a few times. To exist at all, it is dependent upon some other attitude, for it is essentially critical—I would even say parasitical. It has been, and can still be, of great value; but it will never provide showers of partridges or abundance of manna for the chosen peoples.

It is a little difficult to define humanism in Mr. Babbitt's terms, for he is very apt to line it up in battle order *with* religion *against* humanitarianism and naturalism; and what I am trying to do is to *contrast* it with religion.

[145]

Mr. Babbitt is very apt to use phrases like "tradition humanistic and religious" which suggest that you could say also "tradition humanistic *or* religious." So I must make shift to define humanism as I can from a few of the examples that Mr. Babbitt seems to hold up to us.

I should say that he regarded Confucius, Buddha, Socrates, and Erasmus as humanists (I do not know whether he would include Montaigne). It may surprise some to see Confucius and Buddha, who are popularly regarded as founders of religions, in this list. But it is always the human reason, not the revelation of the supernatural, upon which Mr. Babbitt insists. Confucius and Buddha are not in the same boat, to begin with. Mr. Babbitt of course knows infinitely more about both of these men than I do; but even people who know even less about them than I do, know that Confucianism endured by fitting in with popular religion, and that Buddhism endured by becoming as distinctly a *religion* as Christianity—recognizing a dependence of the human upon the divine.

And finally, the attitude of Socrates and that of Erasmus toward the religion of their place and time were very different from what I take to be the attitude of Professor Babbitt. How far Socrates believed, and whether his legendary request of the sacrifice of a cock was merely gentlemanly behaviour or even irony, we cannot tell; but the equivalent would be Professor Babbitt receiving extreme unction, and that I cannot at present conceive. But both Socrates and Erasmus were content to remain critics, and to leave the religious fabric untouched. So that I find Mr. Babbitt's humanism to be very different from that of any of the humanists above mentioned.

This is no small point, but the question is a difficult one. It is not at all that Mr. Babbitt has *misunderstood* any of these persons, or that he is not fully acquainted with the civilizations out of which they sprang. On the contrary, he knows all about them. It is rather, I think, that in his interest in the messages of individuals —messages conveyed in books—he has tended merely to neglect the conditions. The great men whom he holds up for our admiration and example are torn from their contexts of race, place, and time. And in consequence, Mr. Babbitt seems to me to tear himself from his own context. His humanism is really something quite different from that of his exemplars, but (to my mind) alarmingly like very liberal Protestant theology of the nineteenth century: it is, in fact, a product—a by-product—of Protestant theology in its last agonies.

I admit that all humanists—as humanists —have been individualists. As humanists, they have had nothing to offer to the mob. But they have usually left a place, not only for the mob, but (what is more important) for the mob part of the mind in themselves. Mr. Babbitt is too rigorous and conscientious a Protestant to do that: hence there seems to be a gap between his own individualism (and indeed intellectualism, beyond a certain point, must be individualistic) and his genuine desire to offer something which will be useful to the American nation primarily and to civilization itself. But the historical humanist, as I understand

[148]

him, halts at a certain point and admits that the reason will go no farther, and that it cannot feed on honey and locusts.

Humanism is either an alternative to religion, or is ancillary to it. To my mind, it always flourishes most when religion has been strong; and if you find examples of humanism which are anti-religious, or at least in opposition to the religious faith of the place and time, then such humanism is purely destructive, for it has never found anything to replace what it destroyed. Any religion, of course, is for ever in danger of petrifaction into mere ritual and habit, though ritual and habit be essential to religion. It is only renewed and refreshed by an awakening of feeling and fresh devotion, or by the critical reason. The latter may be the part of the humanist. But if so, then the function of humanism, though necessary, is secondary. You cannot make humanism itself into a religion.

What Mr. Babbitt, on one side, seems to me to be trying to do is to make humanism—his own form of humanism—work without religion.

For otherwise, I cannot see the significance of his doctrine of self-control. This doctrine runs throughout his work, and sometimes appears as the "inner check." It appears as an alternative to both political and religious anarchy. In the political form it is more easily acceptable. As forms of government become more democratic, as the outer restraints of kingship, aristocracy, and class disappear, so it becomes more and more necessary that the individual no longer controlled by authority or habitual respect should control himself. So far, the doctrine is obviously true and impregnable. But Mr. Babbitt seems to think also that the "outer" restraints of an orthodox religion, as they weaken, can be supplied by the inner restraint of the individual over himself. If I have interpreted him correctly, he is thus trying to build a Catholic platform out of Protestant planks. By tradition an individualist, and jealous of the independence of individual thought, he is struggling to make something that will be valid for the nation, the race, the world.

The sum of a population of individuals, all

ideally and efficiently checking and controlling themselves, will never make a whole. And if you distinguish so sharply between "outer" and "inner" checks as Mr. Babbitt does, then there is nothing left for the individual to check himself by but his own private notions and his judgment, which is pretty precarious. As a matter of fact, when you leave the political field for the theological, the distinction between outer and inner becomes far from clear. Given the most highly organized and temporally powerful hierarchy, with all the powers of inquisition and punishment imaginable, still the idea of the religion is the *inner* control—the appeal not to a man's behaviour but to his soul. If a religion cannot touch a man's self, so that in the end he is controlling himself instead of being merely controlled by priests as he might be by policemen, then it has failed in its professed task. I suspect Mr. Babbitt at times of an instinctive dread of organized religion, a dread that it should cramp and deform the free operations of his own mind. If so, he is surely under a misapprehension.

And what, one asks, are all these millions, even these thousands or the remnant of a few intelligent hundreds, going to control themselves *for*? Mr. Babbitt's critical judgment is exceptionally sound, and there is hardly one of his several remarks that is not, by itself, acceptable. It is the joints of his edifice, not the materials, that sometimes seem a bit weak. He says truly:

It has been a constant experience of man in all ages that mere rationalism leaves him unsatisfied. Man craves in some sense or other of the word an enthusiasm that will lift him out of his merely rational self.

But it is not clear that Mr. Babbitt has any other enthusiasm to offer except the enthusiasm for being lifted out of one's merely rational self by some enthusiasm. Indeed, if he can infect people with enthusiasm for getting even up to the level of their rational selves, he will accomplish a good deal.

But this seems to me just the point at which "humanistic control" ends, if it gets that far. He speaks of the basis "of religion and humanistic control" in Burke, but what we should like to know is the respective parts played by religion and humanism in this basis. And with all the references that Mr. Babbitt makes to the rôle of religion in the past, and all the connexions that he perceives between the decline of theology and the growth of the modern errors that he detests, he reveals himself as uncompromisingly detached from any religious belief, even the most purely "personal":

To be modern has meant practically to be increasingly positive and critical, to refuse to receive anything on an authority "anterior, exterior, and superior" to the individual. With those who still cling to the principle of outer authority I have no quarrel. I am not primarily concerned with them. I am myself a thoroughgoing individualist, writing for those who are, like myself, irrevocably committed to the modern experiment. In fact, so far as I object to the moderns at all, it is because they have not been sufficiently modern, or, what amounts to the same thing, have not been sufficiently experimental.

Those of us who lay no claim to being modern may not be involved in the objection, but, as

[153]

bystanders, we may be allowed to inquire where all this modernity and experimenting is going to lead. Is everybody to spend his time experimenting? And on what, and to what end? And if the experimenting merely leads to the conclusion that self-control is good, that seems a very frosty termination to our hunt for "enthusiasm." What is the higher will to *will*, if there is nothing either "anterior, exterior, or superior" to the individual? If this will is to have anything on which to operate, it must be in relation to external objects and to objective values. Mr. Babbitt says:

To give the first place to the higher will is only another way of declaring that life is an act of faith. One may discover on positive grounds a deep meaning in the old Christian tenet that we do not know in order that we may believe, but we believe in order that we may know.

This is quite true; but if life is an act of faith, in what is it an act of faith? The Life-Forcers, with Mr. Bernard Shaw at their head, would say I suppose "in Life itself"; but I should not accuse Mr. Babbitt of anything so silly as that.

[154]

However, a few pages further on he gives something more definite to will: it is civilization.

The next idea, accordingly, to be examined is that of civilization. It seems, on the face of it, to mean something definite; it is in fact, merely a frame to be filled with definite objects, not a definite object itself. I do not believe that I can sit down for three minutes to will civilization without my mind's wandering to something else. I do not mean that civilization is a mere word; the word means something quite real. But the minds of the individuals who can be said to "have willed civilization" are minds filled with a great variety of objects of will, according to place, time, and individual constitution; what they have in common is rather a habit in the same direction than a will to civilization. And unless by civilization you mean material progress, cleanliness, etc.—which is not what Mr. Babbitt means; if you mean a spiritual and intellectual coördination on a high level, then it is doubtful whether civilization can endure without religion, and religion without a church.

FOR LANCELOT ANDREWES

I am not here concerned with the question whether such a "humanistic" civilization as that aimed at by Professor Babbitt is or is not *desirable;* only with the question whether it is *feasible.* From this point of view the danger of such theories is, I think, the danger of collapse. For those who had not followed Mr. Babbitt very far, or who had felt his influence more remotely, the collapse would be back again into humanitarianism thinly disguised. For others who had followed him hungrily to the end and had found no hay in the stable, the collapse might well be into a Catholicism *without* the element of humanism and criticism, which would be a Catholicism of despair. There is a hint of this in Mr. Babbitt's own words:

The choice to which the modern man will finally be reduced, it has been said, is that of being a Bolshevist or a Jesuit. In that case (assuming that by Jesuit is meant the ultramontane Catholic) there does not seem to be much room for hesitation. Ultramontane Catholicism does not, like Bolshevism, strike at the very root of civilization. In fact, under certain conditions that are already partly in sight, the Catholic Church may perhaps be the only institution left in the Occident that can be counted upon to uphold civilized standards. It may also be possible, however, to be a thorough-going modern and at the same time civilized. . . .

The last sentence somehow seems to me to die away a little faintly. But the point is that Mr. Babbitt seems to be giving away to the Church in anticipation more than would many who are more concerned with it in the present than he. Mr. Babbitt is much more ultramontane than I am. One may feel a very deep respect and even love for the Catholic Church (by which I understand Mr. Babbitt means the hierarchy in communion with the Holy See); but if one studies its history and vicissitudes, its difficulties and problems past and present, one is struck with admiration and awe certainly, but is not the more tempted to place all the hopes of humanity on one institution.

But my purpose has been, not to predict a bad end for Mr. Babbitt's philosophy, but to point out the direction which I think it should follow if the obscurities of "humanism" were

cleared up. It should lead, I think, to the conclusion that the humanistic point of view is
auxiliary to and dependent upon the religious
point of view. For us, religion is of course
Christianity; and Christianity implies, I think,
the conception of the Church. It would be not
only interesting but invaluable if Professor
Babbitt, with his learning, his great ability, his
influence, and his interest in the most important
questions of the time, could reach this point.
His influence might thus join with that of
another philosopher of the same rank—Charles
Maurras—and might, indeed, correct some of
the extravagances of that writer.

Such a consummation is impossible. Professor Babbitt knows too much; and by that
I do not mean merely erudition or information
or scholarship. I mean that he knows too many
religions and philosophies, has assimilated their
spirit too thoroughly (there is probably no one
in England or America who understands early
Buddhism better than he) to be able to give
himself to any. The result is humanism. I believe that it is better to recognize the weaknesses

[158]

of humanism at once, and allow for them, so that the structure may not crash beneath an excessive weight; and so that we may arrive at an enduring recognition of its value for us, and of our obligation to its author.

THE END